Song for Emilia

Julia Osborne

ETT Imprint
IN ASSOCIATION WITH
Paper Horse Design & Publishing
2017

Song for Emilia is a work of fiction. Names, characters, places, and incidents are the products of the author's imagination or are used in a fictitious manner. Any resemblance to actual events, locales, or persons, living or dead, is entirely coincidental.

Published 2017 by ETT Imprint
in association with Paper Horse Design & Publishing

Copyright © 2017 Julia Osborne
All rights reserved.

National Library of Australia Cataloguing-in-Publication entry:
Osborne, Julia, author
Song for Emilia / by Julia Osborne.
ISBN 9780648096313 (pbk.)
9780648096306 (ebk.)
Romance fiction,
Pianists—Fiction
A823.4

Set in Adobe Garamond Pro 11.5/15pt by Rosie Sutherland for Paper Horse
Titles: Wednesday Sutherland — Musical motifs: Julia Osborne
www.paperhorsedesign.com.au

For my mother, Joy Osborne, who would have enjoyed the saga of the midnight pianist.

With love

Intro:

Sandra remembered it clearly – that fantastic summer day in 1962 when Nick arrived in Sydney to enrol at university.

At the end of the long drive from Curradeen, at last he'd turned the corner into her street, swinging his dusty ute to park at the kerb in front of her house. He slammed shut the ute door, brushed a hand over his hair before clamping on his felt hat and strolling to the front door – ajar on that hot, sticky day.

As he raised a hand to knock, her heart skipping a beat, Sandra reached the door first. Almost sixteen and feeling brave, she'd said hello and kissed his cheek, delighted to have his quick kiss on her forehead in response. Old friends…

She had led him through the house to the back garden where the family sat in the shade of an old tree. Nick Morgan – hers for today, and she knew that it was herself that he'd come to see. Wasn't it?

♪

one.

Two years later, the first day of her Bachelor of Music degree: as Sandra crossed Macquarie Street and walked past the tall, imperious bronze rider on horseback, she could hardly believe her footsteps were taking her to this building. At the front, four crenellated towers like a castle. This was the Sydney Conservatorium of Music: the castle of her dreams and object of her ambition for so many years.

The first time Sandra played in concert, she had been overwhelmed, but managed to complete the performance of her composition to the professor's satisfaction. Tutors encouraged her, 'Talent, hard work and lots of luck,' they insisted. And dedication! Sandra knew she had plenty of that. She'd learned to enjoy playing piano in ensembles – composing for the students with their violins and cellos.

Although her passion for concert performances had fizzled, the fire to compose burned stronger than ever.

By now, Nick was almost halfway through his degree in architecture at Sydney Uni. How many times have we met in those two years? Working it out, she ruefully calculated, makes a total of four or five times a year, plus an occasional lucky phone call from the university college.

Hardly a boyfriend. But she was sure Nick didn't have anyone special. Even though he was five years older, if he was seeing another girl he wouldn't spend any time at all with her. So what did five years matter?

One of those lucky telephone days, she'd hear Nick's voice on the phone with surprised delight:

'G'day, Sandra.'

'G'day,' she'd reply, trying not to giggle. Holding the receiver close to her ear, she'd hear his breath in the phone as if he considered what to say. Usually a suggestion to meet somewhere: coffee at a café, a stroll through the Domain to the Art Gallery. Or after the pictures, they'd go down to Harry's Cafe de Wheels in Woolloomooloo for a pie and mushy peas. They'd sit on the edge of the wharf, feet dangling over the water, revelling in the city lights, the slap of waves against the pilings; their freedom.

Since Sandra had first shown Nick the treasure of Rowe Street's arty shops and galleries, the wonderful bookshop and Rowe Street Records, they'd sometimes met at the Teapot Café. But the café had closed so now they went to the Galleria Espresso, a popular coffee shop for artists, and more comfortable, they agreed, than the Teapot's iron chairs. It was always busy, the walls crowded with paintings, many for sale – painted, they supposed, by the art students that came for coffee, or to sit reading for hours. Who said that life was measured out in coffee spoons, she wondered, stirring another lump of sugar into her coffee.

During uni holidays when Nick went home to Wilga Park, Sandra burned with envy because her best friend Emilia went home for holidays too. They were sure to have struck up a friendship now that Emmy boarded at his grandparents' home in Melbourne while she studied physiotherapy. Not only would Emilia see Nick in Curradeen, but whenever he visited his grandparents.

Mr and Mrs Ferrari were very pleased with this arrangement for their daughter, and although they missed her on the little vegetable patch they called a farm, she was able to train, with a safe place to live.

Emilia knew very well that Sandra had adored Nick since her first year in high school when he was a distant senior, her every step beating time with his name: *Nick Nick Nicholas Nick*. Was it possible that Emmy could somehow infiltrate the Morgan family, and Nick might begin to care for her, instead of Sandra?

Perhaps she sent out feelings to Nick that she wasn't aware of – feelings that suggested, Come this close, and no closer. Perhaps her crush on the piano teacher, Mister L'estrange, had put a spell on her. But Eric L'estrange fell in love with her Aunt Meredith, and Meredith fell in love with him, and Oh, how Sandra had resented it.

Meredith had always been a shining light in Sandra's life: her confidante; someone to run to when there was trouble, which was often enough. It was hard to accept that her Saturday morning excursions with Auntie had gradually disappeared.

At night, lying awake in bed with her arm cradling the pillow, Sandra longed for the touch of Nick's lips on hers. Couldn't he tell? What if she tilted up her face, just as he was about to kiss her forehead – would he dare to kiss her on the lips, even accidentally? Maybe he'd flinch with shock, embarrassed. Oh, horrible thought. But why didn't he ever hold her hand? Such a nice country boy, so well-mannered, her mother had said.

Drifting into sleep, she imagined Nick striding towards her: his long, lean body, felt hat crammed on his head; the big smile. When he talked about life on Wilga Park, his grey-green eyes had a faraway look, and she pondered how deep his love might be for the family property.

… All our lives have changed, she thought, wriggling into a more comfortable position. I bet Nick goes to a pub with his uni mates. At the pub he'll still be the Nick who grew up with Angus – mad as a cut snake, someone called him when they'd got drunk at Morgans' party. Different to the Nick that I know.

Now Angus was dead from the night they crashed the ute on the road to Curradeen, and Nick spent several months in a wheelchair. But Nick won the argument with his father to leave Wilga Park, and was following his dream.

Those final mad, tumultuous weeks had faded away when Emilia arrived for Christmas holidays, bringing a letter from Nick. As Sandra read his few words to say he'd be in Sydney to enrol at university and would visit her, she'd revelled in the idea of seeing him again, conjuring up all the old dreams… her passion for the piano; and the song for Nick that she'd struggled to compose. Shaded with colourful memories of Nick and her visit to Wilga Park, she'd called it *Winter's Day*.

7

At last, here he was: sitting opposite her in the café, stirring several sugars into his tea, felt hat and jacket slung on the back of his chair, shirt sleeves rolled up, the corners of his mouth tipped in a smile.

Gathering her courage, Sandra took the score for *Winter's Day* from her handbag, laid the pages on the table. 'I wrote this for you.' She gave it a little push towards him. 'I designed the title too.'

Nick raised his eyebrows quizzically, drew the score closer. For a moment he contemplated the filigreed title, flicked to the second page, then he said quietly, 'Thank you, Sandra. It's very nice.'

Nice, she thought. Is that all he can say? I've wanted to write that song for so long. For so long I've had it in my head, wanted it to be as perfect as possible to give to Nick, and all he says is—

'It's really nice,' Nick repeated. 'No one ever wrote me a song before.'

That was an improvement. Pacified, Sandra tried to smile more enthusiastically, pleased that he even half-way liked it. 'You read music, so you can play it at the college. There must be pianos there?'

Nick ran a finger along the bars, hummed the first notes. 'I like how it begins—'

Sandra nodded. 'It's Wilga Park,' she said. 'I tried to describe the paddocks in the early morning when you ride Toffee to round up the sheep, and how the sun shines on the frost. See there…' she pointed to the second page, 'that repeated staccato phrase is hoof beats—'

'It's a pretty special present,' Nick chuckled. 'From the pretty piano player. You're a clever girl.'

She laughed with delight; the old nickname he gave me – he hasn't forgotten. Nick went on: 'And I can imagine a day at home just like that. You know, sometimes I miss being there, working with my father – mustering the sheep for shearing, and the lambing, Dad and his precious stud books, the sale yards and his temper if the prices weren't high enough.'

He carefully folded the score, slipping it into his pocket. 'I'm going to order another pot of tea for us,' he said. 'I'm dry as a bone.'

Too soon it was time to leave – they both had study and assignments due. Sandra knew that no matter how long they sat together in a café, wherever they wandered, it always ended the same: Nick would briefly take her hand, then he'd kiss her forehead, right on the spot that had first turned her legs to jelly.

'Goodbye,' Nick was saying. He patted his pocket. 'Thanks again for my song.' And with that swift, endearing kiss, he was striding towards the bus stop.

♪

two.

During the first year of their city life in Randwick, the quest for a job in a florist shop, perhaps even a shop of her own, had been a highlight for Sandra's mother. Next to Angela's armchair, the magazine rack was stuffed with gardening books and newspapers – job advertisements circled in red.

On Saturday mornings, off she would go, *Herald* classified pages in her handbag, to visit the possibilities. Debates at the dining table about the profitability of a fresh flower business became so repetitive, Sandra and her younger sister Prue would leave the table at the first opportunity.

However, after twelve months of fruitless excursions, Angela considered shelving the idea. Sandra's father had originally been supportive, if not exactly enthusiastic. 'Perhaps it's a waste of energy,' Don said consolingly. 'It seems to me that jobs in a flower-shop are scarce as hens' teeth.' A long pause, and he added, 'It might be best to give up on a shop of your own, dear. It's not a financial option.'

Sandra suspected it was a relief for both her parents when Angela finally threw all her newspaper clippings into the backyard incinerator.

All this time, Don quietly worked at the bank, returning home to wander the garden in the evening, smoking his pipe on the seat beneath the peach tree. More and more, Sandra noticed that her father kept to himself. He ate his dinner almost in silence, or said, 'Pass me the pepper, please,' or 'Another cup of tea, please dear?'

Later, regarding the family over the top of his newspaper, he would enquire, 'How was your day?' not noticing that sometimes no one said much. He'd sit on the couch with Ginger on his lap, the old cat audibly purring, Don's eyes closed as if he dozed.

Sandra wondered, was he tired, or was he somehow lonely as the family went in different directions in their spare time. Except her father, who had nothing to do outside the bank and occasionally digging the garden with Angela. Did they spend time with each other, or was it always just passing by: knocking elbows in the kitchen, television each night, a quick kiss goodbye as her father left for work? No old friends for dinner, no afternoon tea parties like at the Curradeen bank.

Sometimes after she and Prue went to bed, she heard the mumble of their muted conversation and once, her father's voice, admitting how he missed his regular golf at the Curradeen club and their golfing friends. They shared a bedroom, and now she was old enough to recognize they were not simply parents but grown-ups with their own private lives, quiet and hidden from view – polite on the surface, enigmatic.

If there was nothing interesting on TV and her piano didn't beckon, Sandra went to her room to lie on the bed and read. She ploughed through the more than nine hundred pages of *Forever Amber,* sneaking the novel from Angela's wardrobe – such a surprise when Auntie gave that book to her mother for Christmas – Angela's eyebrows had shot up – all that outrageous carrying on in the days of Charles II. Condemned by the church for the many sexual escapades, the story was fascinating and absorbing and shocking, all at once, especially the terrible description of how Amber St Clair saved her lover from the plague: the disgusting oozing flesh, the cries of 'Bring out your dead.' Fascinating!

Feeding on the story, Sandra's musical compositions developed a sensuous lyricism, a progression of chords that Aunt Meredith declared absolutely *luscious*. Mister L'estrange initially described her pieces as other-worldly and mysterious, and she liked the description.

Prue's library books left scattered in the lounge room were of myths and legends: witchcraft and spells, vanished kings and queens, crimes and medieval torture chambers. Sandra suspected she liked the mystical side of life. She'd sprung Prue quickly hiding a book beneath her mattress, hissing at Sandra, 'Don't tell!'

Sandra snatched the book, holding it away from her sister. 'Ooh, I like the title, a book of lies – that should suit you. Why is it such a big secret?'

'You know what Mum's like. Please don't say anything.'

'Don't be such a baby, of course I won't.' She opened the cover, flipping pages. 'Gosh, it's an old book... Aleister Crowley, whoever that is. What's it about?'

Prue looked perplexed. 'Magic, I think. I don't understand most of it.' She grabbed the book from Sandra. 'But I'm going to find out, you'll see.'

4

'Gee, it's good to get here,' Emilia said. 'That's the longest trip ever, 'cause men were working on the train line halfway from Curradeen. Nine whole hours! Ooh, my bottom's sore from sitting—'

Sandra chipped in with a laugh, 'Come on, I'll show you where you're sleeping,' She lead the way down the hall. 'Prue's given you her room while she stays at a girlfriend's.'

She hoisted Emilia's suitcase onto the bed. A heavy red suitcase with shiny metal clasps – so different from the old brown port Emilia had lugged to school every day. Sandra took in the changes: a different, very pretty, quite grown-up Emilia, with all the characteristics of her dark-haired, dark-eyed Italian parents. Well, she thought, I did once call her Gina Lollobrigida.

Emilia rolled her eyes as she scanned Prue's wall of cut-out photos: Buddy Holly, Johnny O'Keefe in his gold jacket, a handsome Ricky Nelson. 'I like *Elvis the Pelvis* better than all them...' she remarked. 'Mamma calls him a bodgie. He's real dreamy looking, but.'

It was Prue's room and Sandra was irked by Emilia's scornful opinion of her posters. 'They won't keep you awake,' she said. 'Let's get a glass of cordial—'

'I'd rather have tea. Mrs Morgan's mum always makes us a cup of tea when I get home from college.' Swinging her foot Emilia hummed *Return to Sender.*

Sandra put teapot and cups on the kitchen table. After their hugs and cheerful greetings, words were hard to find. So much time had passed – two years since she'd waved goodbye to her friend on the train back to Curradeen – an Emilia loaded with shopping from her first visit to Sydney.

As they drank their tea, she began to wonder if it was a mistake to have invited Emilia to stay after New Year. Their lives were so different now, running along different tracks in different cities. Gradually their regular letters had dwindled to one every few weeks. What was there to write about, anyway?

'Lofty's going to Melbourne uni, did I tell you? He's doing a B.A. and he wants to teach.'

'He'll be a good teacher,' Sandra mused. 'He was always good in school debates and curious about everything.'

Emilia put down her cup. 'I've got some more news,' she said. 'You know how I said once I want to help people – people like Nick after his car accident when he couldn't walk and had to keep going to Melbourne for treatment? When I graduate and go back to Curradeen there'll be a job for me in the new clinic. They said so.'

This was even worse than Emilia living with Nick's grandparents in Melbourne. As long as Nick was in Sydney, at least he and Sandra were in the same city. She tried to look interested as Emilia kept on chatting about her plans.

'Mamma and Pa are very happy about it, because I'll be back home again. Nonna's getting real old now and my brothers have gone to work at Gillespie's, so they're no help.'

'That's good,' Sandra agreed. 'Your parents will be happy.' But I won't, she thought, feeling dismal. Now Emmy would get to see Nick whenever he drove into town on his holidays.

4

Meredith's voice in the phone: 'We're having a party!' Sandra heard her excitement. 'We want you all to come, and Emilia of course. And why not invite Nick?'

'That sounds great, Auntie, but Nick's gone home for the holidays. When's the party?'

Meredith gave her the date and the time. 'Don't bring anything. Oh, a bottle of wine, if your father wants to.'

Angela cheerfully circled the date on the calendar. 'I'll bring a plate,' she insisted, reaching for her recipe book. 'I'll ask Meredith ... I can make vol-au-vents, maybe chicken and mushroom.'

For the party, Sandra planned to do her hair like Ann-Margret in *Viva Las Vegas*, long and wavy, nothing too big, but Emilia back-combed her black hair very high and sprayed it till it set like varnish, leaving the back to sit stiffly on her shoulders.

'We'll wear our shifts and heels,' they decided, spreading their clothes on the bed. Sandra looked with surprise as Emilia pushed her feet into stilettos. 'How come your mother lets you wear heels that high?'

'Mamma doesn't know.' Emilia gave a cheeky laugh, squirming into her dress. 'And I've got long hems for the farm and short hems for Melbourne. Remember how last visit I made my skirts shorter, then I let them down to go home?' She turned to the mirror, glancing over her shoulder at the back of her dress. 'It's got tight on my bottom,' she admitted. 'Well, too bad, it can't be helped.'

Sandra dug around in the wardrobe and found her kitten heels. They would have to do; there wasn't time to shop for another pair.

Several cars were already parked along the block. Don regarded Emilia's pale frosted lipstick, her eyes outlined in black. 'She looks ill,' he confided to Angela. But Angela shushed him, whispering, 'It's the fashion!'

'She's growing into a little bombshell,' Don laughed. 'Old man Ferrari better watch out.'

Before they reached Meredith's gate, they heard the piano, the hubbub of voices. A string of coloured lights decorated the front porch, the crowded hallway lit by candles. Furniture was pushed back to the walls, the rugs rolled up; so many new faces... friends of Mister L'estrange? Sandra had never met Meredith's friends – their outings had always been just the two of them.

Emilia's face glowed with excitement as she surveyed the room. 'Gee,' she exclaimed, 'I've never been to a real big party.'

Meredith and Mister L'estrange were playing a duet, crossing their hands over, mixing the parts, till Meredith laughing, said, 'That's it, I'm going to see about supper. Keep playing, I can hear in the kitchen.'

Instead, Eric slipped a record onto the turntable, calling, 'Hey, everybody, Chubby Checkerrrr! Let's liven up the joint.'

He jumped to the middle of the room, immediately surrounded by dancers, their hips, knees and elbows twisting madly. Emilia joined in, careless of her tight dress, while Sandra watched with amusement from where she stood by the record player. When the song was over, someone flicked it to play again, and again the frantic twist filled the room.

Another record began, and she recognized the slow, teasing start to *Mambo Italiano*. She longed for Nick to be with her tonight, to dance with her, and only her. The tempo increased, and in an instant, Mister L'estrange had grabbed her by the hand and pulled her into the noisy throng. Singing to the music, he turned her to-and-fro, until realizing her confusion, he put his arm around her waist, taking her unwilling hand in his.

Over his shoulder, she saw Aunt Meredith, glass in hand, watching the dancers: Meredith stunning in a pencil skirt, a black sleeveless top; jade beads around her neck, red hair drawn into a topknot.

'*Go go Joe…*' he sang happily. 'Meredith looks beautiful tonight, doesn't she?'

When Sandra banged a foot into his shoe, he pulled her tighter. 'Syncopated rhythm,' he said with a wink. She stiffened at the unexpected closeness of his body, and as they danced into the kitchen in time to the final notes, he released his hold, leaving her propped beside the sink as he dashed back to the lounge room.

'Eric's such a good dancer,' Meredith said. 'You did very well, considering.'

Considering what, exactly? Sandra felt she'd looked silly, wished he'd left her alone.

In the crowded kitchen, Angela unwrapped a tea towel from her plate of pastries, putting it with the other supper dishes.

'A bottle of claret for you, Meredith,' Don said, adding the wine to a collection of bottles.

'Thank you both very much.' Meredith retrieved dishes from the oven, setting them among hors d'oeuvres and salads. She poured an orange juice each for Sandra and Emilia, topping their glasses with champagne. 'Oops, you girls… not quite old enough I think?'

'I'll be eighteen in April,' Sandra protested. 'But Emmy won't be eighteen till July.'

'Near enough,' Emilia said. 'No one's going to know.'

Meredith had already turned to the guests, 'Supper's in the kitchen,' she announced. 'Come and get it!'

Auntie's so glamorous, Sandra thought, tasting her wine – no wonder Mister L'estrange is in love with her. Some people were dancing a cha-cha, hips swivelling, Eric changing partners at random, and Sandra saw with interest how Emilia followed his every move, eyes narrowed over the rim of her glass.

'He's gorgeous,' she whispered to Sandra. 'Lucky Meredith. Those black eyes. I can see why you like him. Next to him, other boys are boring—'

Sandra interrupted. 'Not Nick. Nick's never boring.'

'Second-best,' Emilia added rudely. 'Come on, I'm going to get more bubbles.'

Exchanging secret smiles, they quickly filled their glasses with champagne, camouflaged with orange juice.

'What are these little rolled-up bacon things, do you think?' Emilia asked, investigating a plate of savouries.

'Angels on horseback,' a woman answered, helping herself to several.

'Oh, cute!' Seizing one, Emilia popped the entire morsel into her mouth, chewed once, and her eyes and cheeks bulged with horror. Gagging, she abandoned her plate and ran for the bathroom.

Amused, the woman explained: 'Grilled bacon wrapped around a fat little oyster, simply delicious. She'll spit it out, I suppose.'

Slipping back to the lounge room, Emilia smothered a giggle. 'I spewed! That was the worst thing ever—' She pulled a disgusted face, then kicked off her shoes to wiggle and shake among the dancers.

Show-off, Sandra thought, sipping her wine, enjoying the fuzzy sensation that made her light-headed, in a floaty, pleasant way. She wished her parents would dance together like at the Denalbo bush dance, happily twirling around the hall, that lovely night she'd danced for a moment with Nick in a barn dance, changing partners all too soon.

The party became quieter as people helped themselves to supper and moved to the courtyard, dining room, or perched on kitchen stools. Eric was playing piano again – a boogie-woogie *Baby Face*, Meredith sharing the seat.

Past midnight, guests began to depart – waving goodbye, singing into the night as Meredith laughingly called, 'Shsssh, you'll wake the neighbours.'

Sandra couldn't see her parents anywhere – maybe in the courtyard where conversation ebbed and flowed. Emilia was asleep on the couch, face squashed into a cushion.

Into the almost-deserted lounge room Sandra heard the singular sound of violins. No one else was dancing and Meredith and Eric held each other close. His arm around her, Meredith's hand on his shoulder, they stood toe-to-toe, listening for the melody to begin. Then slowly stepping, turning, gliding, their steps mirroring each other's, they danced a tango, Meredith's cheek brushing Eric's as they stepped to the side, to swing around each other, perfectly balanced.

Watching her aunt and Mister L'estrange absorbed in each other's embrace, Sandra wondered at her own indefinable emotion...her impossible desire to dance like this with Nick, nestled against his shoulder, oblivious to the world.

The rhythm changed from the earlier dramatic key to a lighter, yet equally yearning melody, and a couple joined in, woozily improvising. At the end of the record, Eric tipped Meredith back in his arms, kissing her to loud applause.

Emilia sat up, bleary-eyed, her dress with sweaty armholes, hair a dishevelled nest. Sandra fished her shoes from under the couch, then leaving Emilia to thoroughly wake up, she searched for Meredith, determined to reinforce the fact that Auntie and Mister L'estrange were together. Eventually he would move in with her, his books, his paintings; his beloved piano. Vaguely, she wondered where he would give his lessons.

Eric had returned to the piano. Hands loose on his knees, eyes half-shut, he paused as if to consider...then with a little shake of his fingers, he began to play. Slow, slow, repeated *pianissimo* phrases gradually building in a crescendo. Sandra had never heard this piece before, and curious, she joined her aunt beside the piano. With a smile, Meredith put her arm around her, cuddled her close. Eric flung them a grin as he theatrically rippled the notes. His foot rhythmical on the pedal, the melody rose and fell, now treble, now bass, at times his right hand suspending the beat. The pianissimo phrases returned, built again in a crescendo that unbidden, carrying her back to the long-ago day she lay alone and dreaming on his bed. He was in England, she was only there to feed the kitten. She'd done her best to forget him – he was Aunt Meredith's. He *loved* Meredith. The delicate aching phrases again, and again the engulfing crescendo. She'd been stupid ... stupid, stupid stupid. Deliberate big chords, the repeated phrases ... she'd meant nothing to him – his pupil, a kid, nothing more. No, she wasn't jealous, Sandra had insisted so many times ... she was over her crush, grown up. Emilia had said he was gorgeous – well yes, she thought so too, and what was wrong with that? Angrily shaking her head, she closed her eyes as with a final crescendo fading to softness, the music ended.

'You're brilliant, darling,' Meredith kissed the top of Eric's head, her hand on his cheek. 'That was delicious.'

'Time to go, I think we're the last to leave.' Don and Angela already waited at the door. 'Simply lovely party, Meredith dear,' Angela said, as Emilia tottered beside them, and Sandra kissed Meredith goodbye, avoiding Mister L'estrange, lest by some weird design, he guessed how his music had affected her.

Don closed the gate with a soft click. Behind them, as they walked to the car, the coloured lights switched off, returning the street to lamp-lit shadows.

From down the hallway where Emilia lay asleep in Prue's bedroom, Sandra could hear her snores.

Dawn lit the sky before she finally slept, and it seemed like only five minutes passed before the sun poked an irritating light through the slats of her venetian blind.

Angela knocked on the door. 'Wakey wakey, rise and shine...' Regardless of Sandra's closed eyes, she flipped open the blind and sat on the bed. 'What a lovely party – we had so much fun, didn't we?'

Sandra rolled over, squinting through slit eyes. 'Muuum, do we have to wake up? It's too early.'

'It's eight o'clock. We want to take you girls on a picnic. Emilia's leaving tomorrow, and we should do something special for her last day.'

'Ask Emmy. Maybe she'd rather do something else...maybe just with me.'

Sandra pulled the sheet over her face, and waited for her mother to get up and leave the room. She knew Emilia wanted to go to the beach again – she wouldn't want to go on a picnic with Sandra's mother and father – a whole day out, eating sandwiches off plastic plates in a park somewhere? Uuurggh.

A thump came from Prue's room. Unless Emilia had fallen out of bed, she must've got up. Wrapping her dressing gown around her, Sandra went to check.

'Ooh, Sandy, look at my hair!' Emilia made a face at her reflection. 'How ever will I fix it?'

Sandra fingered a stiff hank of lacquered curl. 'Wash it in a hot shower?'

Emilia vanished to the bathroom, to emerge some time later with her hair wrapped in a towel.

'You look very regal, Emmy,' Sandra giggled. 'Nefertiti, the queen of Egypt.'

Emilia didn't reply, but took off the towel and began to laboriously comb out the tangle.

After watching the torture for a couple of minutes, Sandra took her comb, saying, 'Here, let me try.' Slowly and carefully, she combed the damp hair, occasionally pulling a strand, with an Ouch! from Emilia.

'Do you want to go to the beach?' Sandra asked. 'Mum said they want to take us on a picnic.'

Emilia was crestfallen. 'Do we have to? It's my last chance to go to the beach for a while.'

'I told Mum you'd rather go out, the two of us, okay?'

After breakfast, they gathered their hats and swimmers, taking a tote bag with towels and a bottle of suntan oil, Jackie Kennedy sunglasses perched on their noses. Angela drove them to Bronte, telling them to sit under the shady trees and not to get sunburnt.

'Don't get sunburnt!' repeated Emilia. 'That's *exactly* what I want...I want to get tanned all over, not all patchy like when I worked in Pa's vegie garden.'

To Sandra's surprise, Emilia wore a bikini. Although she was slimmer, her curves nevertheless overflowed slightly, and she constantly hitched at the top.

'I bet your father doesn't know you wear that,' Sandra said. Her own bikini was more like a two piece, and definitely more secure.

'Shit no! Pa would rather I wore black, neck-to-knee.' Emilia screwed up her nose, reaching for the suntan oil bottle.

Slathered in coconut oil they raced into the water, dodging among bathers, Emilia immediately disappearing under a wave, to emerge grabbing at her top as it threatened to slide off.

'Golly,' she said. 'I better watch out or I'm going to lose something.'

Sandra noticed that several young men were watching them. The first swim Emilia had at Bondi two years ago, she'd flirted enthusiastically with the boys who swam around them both, but today she wasn't interested, flinging the group a scornful glance.

'Idiots, they're only looking at my bikini.'

'And the rest!' Sandra said. 'Every time you come up from a wave, you look like you'll lose your top. They're all waiting.'

'They'll be disappointed,' Emilia sniffed, and returning to their towels, she pulled on a tee-shirt, smirking at the young men as she dived back into the surf.

Later as they lay in the sun, Emilia said, 'I drank a lot of bubbles last night. Did you, too?'

'Not like you.' Sandra spread oil on her arms and legs, smearing more oil onto Emilia's back. 'You looked really tipsy when you went to sleep on the couch.'

'How embarrassing,' Emilia sighed. 'But it was a fantastic party. 'Ooh, Mister L'estrange is so divine. No wonder you've got a crush—'

'No, I don't any more,' Sandra said emphatically. 'He's with Auntie now, and they're madly in love.'

'That's obvious. Maybe they'll have beautiful babies.'

'Gosh, I hadn't thought of that. Isn't she too old?

'Back where my parents come from, even old ladies in their forties have babies.'

'That's Italy – maybe they can't get the Pill over there.'

It was an interesting notion: Aunt Meredith with a baby? But first Sandra had to get used to the idea of them being together, and Mister L'estrange hadn't moved in yet.

'Let's get an icecream?' Sandra was on her feet already, sunhat jammed on her wet hair. 'I can feel my skin getting tight, I know I'm burning.'

The little shop was busy and they waited to be served, the pavement getting increasingly hot under their sandals. Running into the park, they sighed with relief to lick their rapidly melting icecream cones under the trees.

After dinner they sat in the garden trickling the hose over their feet. Sandra touched Emilia's shoulder. 'You've gone really red. Does it hurt?'

'A bit. That tomato didn't do any good. My back feels worse.'

'Mine too. We'll put on some baby oil before bed.'

'I love Bondi and Bronte,' Emilia said. 'Where I live now, I can only go to the local pool, and that's not so much fun.'

'Do you like living there?'

'Yep. I like Mrs Morgan's parents – they're real nice to me. Pa wouldn't have let me go to Melbourne if I didn't have somewhere good to stay. I like my course, and it's not too far to go home for holidays.'

As Emilia spoke, it wasn't hard to feel jealous, but Sandra brushed it off. Nick had returned to Wilga Park after his exams… it was weeks since she'd seen him. He'd almost become a dream, leaving a little hole in her heart.

'Lucky thing, to live away from home,' she said. 'Do you go out much?'

'Not much, just sometimes to the pictures with girl friends.'

'I'll miss you when you go tomorrow. At school, my only real friend was Carol, and now she's at teachers' college I don't see her much. I know a few students at the Con – there's a nice boy called Billy studying saxophone—'

'Ooh,' Emilia crowed, eyes narrowed. 'A nice boy called *Billy*?'

'He's just in my year, so don't get any ideas. He's keen to play in a club and he asked if I'd be interested.'

Sandra's best friend at the Conservatorium had turned out to be Billy. She liked his easy company, their talk always about music. The idea of a duo was tempting.

'What's he look like?'

'He's very tall with sort of ginger hair—'

'Urk, a carrot-top… he's probably all freckly.' Emilia dismissed him with a laugh. 'Remember the pact we made?'

'Of course I do,' Sandra replied. 'To always be best friends, for ever and ever – boys excluded.'

'So, what about you and Nick?'

While she wondered how to answer this delicate question, Sandra looked across the garden. Her mother's beans had raced up the wire trellis, and along the fence she'd grown tall flowering plants with forgettable names. So many seed packets littered the kitchen bench – delphiniums, maybe.

She hosed a mosquito off her leg. 'I don't know. I wish I could see him more often. We go to a café now and then, or to the pictures, that's about all.'

It sounded very threadbare to Sandra. Well, that was about all, wasn't it, she told herself. Nick was like a shadow, only visible when the sun shone, and it didn't shine often enough for her.

Angela called them through the kitchen window: 'Dinner's on the table, girls.'

As they stood up, their clothes pulled on their sunburnt skin. 'Gosh,' Sandra said. 'We're going to peel and look terrible.'

'No, we won't,' Emilia grinned, flicking newly silken curls off her face. 'We'll look like two water-babies who had a wonderful day at the beach.'

Dinner was quiet, and both Sandra and Emilia felt sleepy soon after they finished.

'Off you go,' Angela said. 'I'll let you off the washing-up tonight.'

Despite Sandra's worries, Emilia's visit had ended peacefully, all their chatter bridging whatever gaps had opened between them. They hugged goodnight, but instead of immediately going to bed, they lay beside each other on the top sheet, talking about everything they'd already talked about a hundred times, until Angela whispered at the door that it was nearly midnight.

They kissed goodnight, and Emilia touched the small china angel on the dressing table – her present to Sandra two Christmases ago. 'My little angel will look after you while you're asleep.'

'She's the first thing I see when I wake up,' Sandra replied sleepily. 'I love my little angel.'

'Sssh,' came Angela's voice again, from down the hallway.

Tomorrow the train would whisk Emilia off to Curradeen – the long journey home to stay with her family before the study year began.

Eyes closed, vaguely dreaming, Sandra heard the regular rhythm of the train as it picked up speed on the tracks to the western line, Emilia's handkerchief waving out the window…

Goodbye, goodbye.

4

Blue sky and a bright March sun gave the day a holiday feel, although it was only a weekend.

Prue's face wore a grumpy expression as she plumped down on Sandra's bed. 'How come you never want to do anything with me, anymore,' she complained. 'You had plenty of time when Emilia was here.'

Sandra didn't look up from her desk. 'I'm working, go away.'

Prue ignored her rebuke. 'Not even draughts or Scrabble—'

'Are you deaf?' Really, Prue could be tiresome…

'We never ride our bikes anywhere, even when—'

'Ha, you've crashed your bike three times already and gone to hospital. No wonder Dad locked up your bike. All you do now is hang about with your girlfriends and go to the Stadium.'

'At least I'm having fun. Better than you stuck at home all weekend scribbling songs. Monopoly, one game?'

'I don't want to play Monopoly. Or any game.' Head bent over her score again, Sandra tried to recollect where she'd got up to. It was already a difficult composition.

When Sandra continued to ignore her, Prue said, 'I'm getting the bus out to The Gap. Want to come with me?'

Sandra didn't immediately answer. It wasn't too far in the bus to Watson's Bay, and it would save her from her desk for the day. The invitation had a certain appeal.

'All right, let me finish this.'

Prue stretched out on the bed, hands behind her head, jiggling her foot. 'It's funny,' she said, 'but even though I've got plenty to do and I've got heaps of friends, I sort of miss how we used to ride our bikes out to the creek.'

Sandra was surprised by this admission of sentiment from Prue, usually so self-contained. 'I miss it too,' she confessed. 'Emilia's still my best friend, but I don't see anyone much now I've left school.'

'I liked how sometimes we caught yabbies. Remember?'

'Yes, and then we'd let them go.'

'You used to feed those horses and pretend they were yours.'

'Mmm,' Sandra mumbled, concentrating on her melodic line.

Prue picked through the books on the bedside table. She held one up. 'What's this about?'

A quick glance, and Sandra said, 'Mendelssohn's life story, you wouldn't like it. Now, will you be quiet?'

Prue hummed to herself, reading a page. 'It says here his sister Fanny – that's a funny name – composed songs and she played piano, too.'

'So did Mozart's sister. Shut up for five minutes.'

Prue sighed. 'I'm supposed to work harder at school...I wish I could've left after the Intermediate.'

'Don't be a wimp.'

'Look who's talking.'

With an exaggerated sigh, Sandra folded the score with its squiggly quavers, crochets and chords, and dropped her pencil into the box. 'There's nothing wimpy about studying at the Con – we don't just sit around and play tunes all day.'

As if Sandra hadn't spoken, Prue said: 'In class yesterday, I had to read Lady Macbeth's part, where she says...if she'd sworn to do it, she'd tear her baby's mouth off her nipple and dash his brains out. *Nipple!* I had to read *nipple*. I bet all the kids were glad it was me and not them.'

Sandra laughed, imagining Prue's unaccustomed embarrassment. At least a bus trip to The Gap was something different. Her life had been strangely quiet since Aunt Meredith and Mister L'estrange fell in love.

The bus emptied many of its passengers near the harbour-side beaches, then continued up the hill and along the road towards The Gap.

At first they leaned their elbows on the fence. Beyond, the cliffs dropped down down and down to the rocks below. Sandra felt a creepy sensation knowing that this was a favourite place for sad, desperate people to jump to their deaths. Or be pushed. A year ago when they'd first visited The Gap together and leaned on the fence like today, Prue admitted to enjoying this feeling – the thrill of anticipation, imagining the leap...

'I'm climbing the fence,' Prue said. 'My favourite pozzy's over there.' She pointed southwards, to a narrow sandstone ledge beyond the ragged cliff-top grass and wind-beaten bushes.

Projecting a short distance from the cliff face, it filled Sandra with horror. 'Don't,' she pleaded. 'It looks too dangerous.'

'I've often done it.' Prue slipped through the fence. 'Be a sook if you want to.' She walked along the cliff top, to sit on the stone ledge, feet hanging over the sea.

Cross at the old accusation, Sandra followed her, hands and feet tingling with apprehension. Aunt Meredith would be appalled. As for her parents – their mother would have a heart attack. This thought gave her a false courage, and she sidled over to sit beside Prue. Far below the waves frothed dark and fathomless against the darker rocks. Perhaps it would seem less menacing when morning sunlight sparkled on the cliff face, lighting its colours. If she stared down into it long enough, would it would begin to beckon...was that what people called vertigo?

For a while they sat in silence, swinging their legs as they watched the swell gush in and out among the rocks.

'What's it like to jump off, do you think?' Prue asked. 'You'd have to be a bit mad, wouldn't you?'

Sandra contemplated the question. Aunt Meredith had described how her boyfriend William had been a bit mad when he came back from the Korean War, but he hadn't meant to get run over. Auntie told her how William had nightmares, and walked the streets around Bronte half the night – till he got hit by a tram in the early dawn light. It was an accident, wasn't it? She hated how her own questions bounced back at her.

Before she could answer Prue, behind them, somewhere back on the road, they heard a voice call. It called again, urgent: 'Hey, you! You girls!'

Turning her head, Sandra saw a man hurrying across the road towards them, his voice more anxious with every step.

'Come off that cliff, girls. Quickly and quietly now.' He stood at the fence, hands on hips.

He seemed so worried, Sandra said, 'Something's up. We'd better do as he says.'

Prue gave a snort, but inched back from the edge, swinging her feet onto the grass. They climbed back through the fence, to stand regarding the man whose face showed immense relief.

'What on earth—' he began. 'It's sandstone, don't you know? A soft stone. Where you were sitting, bold as brass enjoying the afternoon sun, the weather can eat out the stone underneath, wearing it away. Sometimes big chunks can suddenly fall into the sea.' His face softened with relief. 'Please, will you never, never do that again.'

Sandra shivered as she understood what he meant. She looked back at the ledge where they'd sat, saw how the wind and weather had begun to wear a hollow beneath it. Maybe in years to come, or maybe tomorrow, that ledge would crack, tumbling broken rocks down into the sea.

As they walked back to the bus stop, 'How would he know?' Prue scowled. 'Silly old man.'

'He lives over the road, so he'd know,' Sandra replied. 'Maybe he watches everything, to save people from jumping off The Gap. Anyway, I believe him.'

'Maybe he thought we'd made a suicide pact,' Prue said. 'Hold hands. Jump off the cliff together.'

Sandra glanced sideways at her sister. 'You say such stupid things.'

But later she worried, listening to the records Prue played in her bedroom, the portable turntable spinning songs of loss and anguish. *Heartbreak Hotel* ad infinitum.

♪

three.

Don and Angela returned to their comfortable armchairs after dinner. When *Rawhide* finished, the house relaxed in a mood of peace and quiet: a beautiful evening, warm enough for cicadas to sing. Tonight there wasn't any argument about whose turn to wash or dry the dishes, and washing up done, Sandra and Prue went to their bedrooms to read or finish homework.

Don breathed out a little cloud of smoke, tapping his pipe on the ashtray. 'Since we moved to Sydney, we've spent all our holidays at home. I've been thinking maybe we should do something different.'

'Now we live near the beach, it's not as if—'

'Angela, dear,' Don said, 'it hasn't been easy for me. You know the new branch is a big workload, and it'll get worse with decimal currency coming in '66. I'd like to get out of the city at least for part of my holiday, breathe some bush air again for a week or so.'

'What do you have in mind?'

'We can drive down the coast, then go inland to Adaminaby and Lake Eucumbene. The whole Snowy hydro scheme will be fun to visit and an education for the girls. The lake must have filled by now. We can camp, or stay in cabins or a motel. How about it?'

'I'll leave it for you to investigate,' Angela said. Really, she would rather stay at home. The garden needed attention – the new zucchinis might die in her absence. Disappointed at the thought, she agreed. 'It sounds a very nice idea.'

In her nightdress, Sandra came from the kitchen with a glass of milk. 'What sounds a nice idea?'

'Your father wants to take us on a holiday to Lake Eucumbene, before school goes back.'

'Why do we want to go to some old lake out in the country? We can have our holiday at home,' Sandra said, innocently echoing her mother's opinion.

'It's a new lake,' Don said. 'Part of the grand Snowy Mountains scheme for hydro-electricity. You've heard how to make way for the dam, almost every building in Adaminaby, even a church, was moved by truck or picked apart and rebuilt brick by brick and stone by stone. Now the lake is famous, people can go fishing for trout—'

'Dad, we don't go fishing for trout, or anything, *ever!*' Sandra heard herself whinge. 'I've got things I want to do.'

'Now now,' Angela interrupted. 'Those things will still be here when you get home.'

'Great,' Sandra muttered. 'Drowned houses. Sounds terrific fun.' Then an idea occurred to her, a brilliant idea. Her father would never dream of leaving the cat! 'What about Ginger?' She watched her father's face. 'We can't just leave him alone with bowls of food.'

Don hadn't thought about the cat and he frowned. 'Perhaps we can find someone to mind him,' he suggested, sounding doubtful.

'Why Lake Eucumbene?' Angela asked. 'If you want to go bush for a week, why not go back to Curradeen?'

He hadn't thought of that, either. 'Curradeen? I suppose—'

Suddenly excited, Sandra leaped at the chance. 'That's a great idea, Dad. Why not go back to Curradeen, and I can come with you. The next uni break in June?' *And*, she thought, Nick will be at home too. Nick, at Wilga Park! 'I can stay with Emilia—' her words were falling over themselves.

'You could stay with one of our golfing friends.' Angela got up to fill the kettle, relieved that another option had unexpectedly arisen. 'You know how you miss your golf,' she said. 'Prue and Ginger and I can stay here, and you two can have a nice time in the country.'

Don brightened. 'You're right. I'll take some time off now, and the rest of my leave I'll add to the Queen's birthday weekend. My goodness, a week of golf...' He leaned back in his armchair, satisfied with the outcome.

'Anyway,' he said, as if in conclusion, 'with such a widespread drought, water in the lake might be quite low – all those dead trees poking out of the water.'

Gleeful, Sandra took her glass of milk back to the bedroom. This was getting better and better. She opened the zipped writing case she'd got for Christmas, and took out her pen. A letter to Emilia, plus a letter to Nick: *Dear Nick, my father and I are going on a holiday together, and we'll be coming to Curradeen for a few days over the uni study break. Will you be home then?*

Up at dawn on their day of departure, Sandra shoved an extra pair of socks into her suitcase. Nights in June could be cold out west, so an extra jumper... slacks, skivvies, jeans and desert boots, her beanie. They'd be gone for a week, so better be ready for everything.

Angela was already up and had put breakfast on the table. The kitchen smelled of bacon and eggs.

'Let's eat and hit the road,' Don said with a big smile as he stowed his golf bag in the boot beside their suitcases.

Prue hadn't cared about going to Curradeen, saying she'd rather visit her friends – the 'gang of girls' as her mother called them. Goody, Sandra thought. We've never done anything like this before. Just me and Dad. And Nick at Wilga Park.

The rising sun was behind them as they reached the open road travelling west. Angela had packed a box with morning tea and a thermos, and they knew where to find the best Chinese café for lunch, from their countless journeys to Sydney. It would be dark before they reached their old town.

'Father and daughter, eh?' Don remarked as they left behind the city traffic. 'An adventure.'

Sandra nodded, happy for her father. He loved his golf and hadn't played since they arrived in Randwick. This was going to be better than some silly old lake, she thought. I don't care how important it is or how big it is. We're going to Curradeen, and it's all going to be wonderful.

As the miles ticked over, she recalled her letter to Nick. Their last afternoon together was weeks ago. Now he was home for uni break, and he'd made a suggestion that was so delicious, she took his letter out of her handbag for the sheer pleasure of reading it for the thousandth time.

> Dear Sandra,
>
> Thanks for your letter. It's a great idea for you & your father to visit. I'll be home over the study break. There's a lot for you to see on our place that will be new to you. I'll get Toffee back from where she's agisted & we've got a nice, quiet horse for you, so we'll have that ride I promised.

He'd remembered his promise... at the polocrosse match, at least three years ago – the unforgettable day they'd first met.

> Mum still has the old piano of course, some things don't change, & you can play Winter's Day for us, & maybe

some more of the compositions you've told me about. Have a safe trip, it's a long drive. Don't I know it!

'*Yours, Nick*,' she whispered. Oh Nick, whenever I see you everything seems to go better.

She slid the letter back in its envelope. For a while, they drove in silence, winding up and up the road to the Blue Mountains. The sun was high, and as they arrived in Katoomba, Don said, 'Morning tea time, Sandy. Shall we say hello to the Three Sisters?'

'Oh yes, we always stop there. I like to imagine what it was like when the first explorers crossed it, like Blaxland, Lawson and Wentworth. To walk and walk and suddenly come to that enormous cliff, and a valley, blue as blue.'

Don poured the tea into plastic cups. 'You should write a story about it. Or a song?'

'Yes! A landscape song. The blueness of the valley… I love the line of sandstone cliffs in the distance,' Sandra said, scattering crumbs from a biscuit. 'And I want to write a song for Emilia too, because she's still my best friend.'

'What a nice idea. How's the study going these days?'

'Good. My tutor said now I've done eighth grade piano, I should think about sitting the A.Mus.A. exam – the Associate Diploma in Music.'

'Really? You haven't mentioned it. That's a very good qualification.'

Sandra had been silent on her progress since being accepted at the Conservatorium. Busy with studying piano and composition, she was flying through the work. Restless, she badly wanted to put into practice all she'd learned, and longed to spend the time at her piano – filling her score sheets, filling her box of compositions – unfettered.

'Enrolments for the exam close soon... I'm not sure.' She packed the empty cups back in the box with the thermos. 'I think I'd rather just study.'

'A few days away might help you decide. Talk to Mum and me about it.'

Don started the car and they drove up the hill to the township, and on to the highway. 'Next stop Blayney. Do you think we can find our favourite café again?'

'You know,' he said, the lines around his mouth framing a smile. 'I feel better already. Your mother was right, I needed a holiday!'

A lowering sun dazzled on the windscreen as they began the last long miles of their journey. Wallaby grass grew by the roadside, eucalypts and casuarinas. Drought was creeping across the countryside, and beyond the boundary fences, paddocks were brown with winter grass; here and there the dark shapes of cattle. Soon they would be in sheep country. Soon they would arrive at Curradeen.

7

Don parked at the gate to Ferrari's Farm as Emilia came running out the door, curls bouncing.

Squeezing Sandra tightly, she cried, 'Sandy! I'm so happy you're here, I could burst.'

Mrs Ferrari gathered Sandra into her arms, exclaiming, 'Ooh, look at you, *bella, bella ragazza,* all grown up, such a long time since you visit.' She kissed her on each cheek. 'I miss my girl, too, now she is so clever to study in Melbourne.'

Don shook his head at the offer of a cup of tea, and as they waved goodbye, Emilia took Sandra by the arm. 'Come and say hello to Nonna. She's been waiting to see you, and she's cooked a real nice dinner especially.'

Emilia's grandmother sat in her usual chair in the kitchen, exactly as Sandra remembered her: the same black scarf covered her hair, the familiar long skirt. She put down her knitting with a happy sigh. *'Benvenuta, mia cara.'* Eyes shining, she clasped Sandra to her, adding many more indecipherable words to her greeting.

'She says, Welcome, dear,' Emilia translated. 'Plus some words I couldn't understand, she's very glad you're here.'

'Tell her I still wear the scarf she knitted for my birthday.'

After a voluble translation to her grandmother, Emilia said, 'Now you've got to come and see my bedroom. It's always real messy, but I fixed it up for you.'

The bedroom wasn't as crowded as when Sandra last stayed, and an extra bed easily fitted in. Emilia had tidied away ornaments that previously overflowed from every available space – china animals, toys, comics and holy pictures; bangles and beads. Sandra picked up a framed photo of them both in their school uniforms. 'That was in second year,' she said. 'I was so skinny.'

Emilia sat on the bed, brushing her long, thick gloss of black curls. 'Sit next to me and I'll brush yours, too,' she said. 'I can't believe you're here, and we're going to have so much fun just like we used to do.'

Sandra sat beside her, yielding to the gentle brush. 'Your hair's real pretty,' Emilia said. 'Do you remember my visit to you after the Intermediate, and all those icecreams your auntie bought us? I came home so fat.'

'We ate so many pastries,' Sandra said. 'But now Aunt Meredith's going with Mister L'estrange, I don't do things like that any more.'

As if reading her mind, Emilia asked, 'Do you still like him?'

'You know I don't. That was just dopey. A stupid crush.'

'Ooh, but you were mad about him. He's very attractive, like a gypsy. I'd have gone for him too.' Emilia hugged herself. 'I would've eaten him all up.'

Looking at Emilia curled on the bed – her rosy lips, her round white knees – Sandra didn't doubt it. As for herself, her bedroom mirror informed Sandra that she looked quite pretty, but she felt sure her face was never going to launch a thousand ships, and although she'd grown, she still felt a squib beside other girls.

'So it's all about Nick now?' Emilia persisted.

What could she say? When she phoned Nick to say they'd arrived in town, he'd immediately invited Sandra to visit, and her father would drive her out to Wilga Park in a day or two. Late in the afternoon, Nick would take her back to the Ferrari's. Maybe then, she'd finally discover how Nick felt about her. If not, she might as well forget him.

Emilia continued to tell her stories: 'I told you Lofty's in Melbourne—' When Sandra didn't immediately answer, waiting for more, she said: 'He's nice, now that he's older.'

'He was so annoying the way he followed us around at school, making silly faces.'

'Because he liked you,' Emilia giggled. 'But after you left town, he used to walk me home from school, and he's taller now.'

'Lofty will always be Lofty, even when he wanted to get called Warwick.' Sandra said, tired of hearing about Lofty. 'What about Roger, who worked on your father's vegetable garden?'

'Roger joined the army.' Emilia gave a snort of laughter. 'It was funny how he kissed me when I wasn't looking—'

'How can anyone kiss you when you're not looking?' That was too silly to contemplate, and they collapsed in a fit of giggles.

Emilia borrowed a bicycle for Sandra, and they cycled in all the old, familiar directions: the pioneer cemetery where they wandered among the weather-worn gravestones, and to the creek a few miles out of town, but dry weather had sucked up all the water and only stones remained beneath drooping trees.

'Miss Brooks might be home,' Sandra puffed, as they pedalled back to town on the dirt road. 'I know last time her house looked like she'd gone for good, but can we see?'

On her last visit, Sandra had discovered her unopened letter lay eaten by snails in the letterbox, and only weeds choking the garden. Her old music teacher was such a treasure, and Sandra had been deeply disappointed not to be able to talk about her new teacher, perhaps even to play a new piece for her.

They cycled along the road leading to the row of weatherboard cottages. The front door was open, letting in morning sunshine. Poppies flowered scarlet, pink and yellow along the path to the veranda. Miss Brooks was at home!

'Dear lass,' Miss Brooks spoke in her soft northern English accent as she embraced Sandra. 'I said I'd never go back because all my family there were dead, but you know, that's just what I did – one last visit to my old home.'

Sandra and Emilia followed her along the hallway, past the music room where she'd taught Sandra for five years, and into the kitchen. Miss Brooks put on the jug to boil, setting out fine china tea cups patterned with roses and violets.

'Now you must tell me what you've been up to,' she said.

As they sipped their tea, Sandra told her about the pieces she'd studied. 'I didn't like my new teacher at first, he was so rude,' she said. 'I kept thinking of you, and wishing you could still teach me.'

'I got lots of letters grumbling about him,' Emilia joined in.

Miss Brooks tut-tutted. 'You're a lovely pianist, Sandra, any teacher would have recognized that.'

'He was so different with his long hair and he's got an earring – it gave Mum a shock – but he's such a good teacher, now she likes him too. And he encourages me to write my own compositions.'

As Sandra rambled on with interruptions from Emilia, Miss Brooks nodded, making a remark now and then: 'I see,' or sometimes, 'Well, well, well.'

Finally, she said, 'You must play for me, Sandra. Why not *Clair de Lune*,' like you played at our concert? I'd love to hear that again. I'll find my music—'

'I don't need the score,' Sandra said. 'Since you taught it to me, I practised and practised.' Settling herself at the familiar piano, Sandra played the quiet opening bars...the brilliant arpeggios unfurling as her fingers flickered up and down the keyboard, to end with an echo of the first pianissimo notes, then the final, wonderful chord.

'I remember that tune,' Emilia cried, breaking the spell.

'Better than ever,' Miss Brooks said. 'Now, dear lass, I must tell you something.'

At Miss Brooks' request, Sandra poured more tea, emptying the pot. Her music teacher smiled, but there was sadness in her face. To Sandra, Miss Brooks had always been old, but today she noticed the deeper lines, and on her neck, veins showed blue beneath her papery skin, as if she was slowly becoming transparent.

'I'm going quite deaf.' Miss Brooks gave a little sigh. 'First it was just my left ear, but now I have great trouble hearing people speak, and I've lost all the top notes in my music.'

Sandra didn't know what to say. Miss Brooks, deaf? Her life had been immersed in music, and now, to lose all that, bit by bit?

So she couldn't have properly heard *Clair de Lune.* Near tears, her throat ached, and she impulsively reached for Miss Brooks' hand, felt the strong, bony fingers return her warmth.

'Could you hear anything of what we said?' Emilia asked.

'A little, my dear,' Miss Brooks answered. 'It's better when only one person talks, but you two, so excited…' her voice trailed off. 'I'm very glad to see you, Sandra, and to know that although you may not want to be the concert pianist you always aspired to being, you are composing your beautiful songs. Play one of those for me now, lass, and Emilia and I will sit quietly and listen.'

♪

four.

Wilga Park... Gosh, Sandra could scarcely believe it as they drove towards the homestead, settled in its garden behind the line of peppertrees. Her hands were sweaty, and she felt a trickle of nervous perspiration under each arm. It's weeks since you've seen Nick, she told herself – crazy to worry about what he thinks or what he feels...

Don glanced at her with a wink as he turned the wheel and the tyres crunched on the driveway. He turned off the ignition. 'Here we are. And there's Nick, waiting for us.'

Nick stood on the veranda, shading his eyes against the morning sun. Sandra glimpsed sun-browned face, tousled hair, the sweater and moleskins, then he'd swung down the steps, full of smiles.

'You made it! Good to see you both.'

Greeting them with a swift shake of her father's hand, Nick dropped a kiss on Sandra's forehead, sending a tiny shock-wave down her spine. She wanted to stare and stare, fall into those grey-green eyes, soak him up. She smiled back at him then tore her gaze away.

He surprised her with a quick hug. 'It's a great day for a ride, and we've got the perfect horse for you.'

Don looked around the garden, appraising the dry conditions. 'Looks like you could do with a drop of rain?'

'It's dried off all right. Farmers need a good fall for the winter wheat.' Nick's glance swept across the garden, the yellow grass. 'An early frost's burned it off.' He led the way to the veranda steps. 'Come on in,' 'Mum's got the kettle on already, I'll bet.'

Mrs Morgan came hurrying out the front door, dusting her hands together. 'I've made scones,' she said. 'You'll stay for a cuppa, Don, won't you?'

4

Nick lifted the stock saddle onto Paddy, the sturdy bay horse he'd brought in for Sandra to ride.

'Paddy's too fat,' he remarked, tightening the girth with difficulty, dodging the horse's playful attempt to knock off his hat. 'He was my first horse. Now he's about twenty-five, and he hasn't done any real work for years, lazy old boy.'

Nick had retrieved Toffee from his friend's farm, and together they would ride out across the home paddocks. 'Maybe we'll go as far as one of the creeks on our place,' Nick said. 'Okay with you?'

Sandra could only nod in agreement, with no idea how a few hours in the saddle would feel, as she'd never ridden a horse before. Hair tied in a bunch on her neck, she wore her jeans, boots, and a sloppy joe, and Nick had found her a felt hat.

'You'll be plenty warm enough,' he said. 'This time of year, it's the nights that are cold.' He held Paddy's bridle, as with her foot in the stirrup, Sandra hauled herself into the saddle. 'Put some weight in the stirrups,' Nick said, adjusting the lengths, 'and don't be nervous. I'll put Paddy on a lead rein till you get used to the saddle.'

They ambled through the home paddocks, on through another gate, leaving behind a chorus of barks from the two working dogs, resigned to their chains today. Paddy was indeed fat, but comfortable to ride – rather like an armchair, she thought – the horse big and solid beneath her.

Trailing behind Toffee with no need to direct the old horse, she could observe Nick, liking the easy way he sat in the saddle, brown curls overlapping the collar of his rough wool coat, the battered felt hat; his hands firm on the reins keeping Toffee at a gentle pace. Now and then he turned to see how she was getting on.

'Toffee's foal just turned three,' he said, letting Paddy come alongside. 'Honey's grown into a beauty, with a nice temperament like her mother. I'll probably sell her – I'm not often here, so there's no point having another horse.'

'Oh, that's sad, selling her.' She remembered on her last visit to Curradeen how she'd unexpectedly run into Nick and his mother in the main street, and his story of the new foal – as yet without a name.

'Maybe you can think of one?' Nick had suggested.

It had burst past her lips, unbidden, miraculously: '*Honey!*' she'd cried.

And Nick had given a thumbs up, saying, 'Perfect for a sweet little foal.'

'Will I get to see her?' she asked.

'We'll see how time goes,' Nick answered, but Sandra guessed that this probably meant *No*.

Dismounting to open another gate, Nick followed a meandering path across a paddock where numerous sheep grazed, fussily nibbling at the short grass. Beyond, rolling acres of saltbush merged with the blue of the sky.

'These are some of Dad's best ewes,' he explained. 'They'll drop their lambs in a few weeks, so I hope we get a decent fall of rain soon.'

He unclipped the lead rein, saying, 'See how you go on your own. Don't worry, Paddy won't take off, he's too lazy, and he'll stick by Toffee.'

Holding the reins the way Nick had showed her, they rode towards a line of trees and presently came to a creek. Nick pulled up his horse in the shade of the casuarinas and swiftly slipped down from the saddle. Sandra swung her right leg over Paddy's rump, but it seemed a long way down and she hesitated to jump.

To her surprise, Nick put his hands around her waist and easily lifted her to the ground. Just like in a film, Sandra thought, except in a film, that's when the boy kisses the girl…

'Your legs might like a rest,' Nick said, securing the horses.

In fact, her legs felt like jelly, and where her jeans had bunched up by the stirrup leathers, little blisters rubbed raw.

'Are there any snakes?' she asked, peering about suspiciously.

'Not this time of year. There's mostly black ones around here, the odd brown.'

Sandra was pleased to hear it, not sure how she would react if she startled a snake.

Nick tossed her an apple from his saddle bag, and they sat on a fallen branch angled toward the creek. Several wood swallows dipped and soared above them. Near some scattered shade trees, two grey kangaroos raised their heads to stare inquisitively, ears twitching. Sandra took off her boots so she could stretch her cramped toes, first adjusting her jeans so that he wouldn't see the sore on each calf.

Nick nodded towards the kangaroos. 'The last of the tribe,' he said. 'Most of the 'roos have moved on although some still hang around the water troughs.' He munched his apple, while the kangaroos resumed their rest. 'How are you getting on with Paddy?'

'I love it. My first ride, and all I ever wanted growing up was to have a horse.'

'Well, Paddy is most honoured.' Nick chucked his apple core, watched it bounce across the gully. 'I've never seen the creek so low. It's a bad sign.'

'What will your father do if it doesn't rain?'

'Move some sheep off the property to better grazing. Apart from his breeders, he'll sell any surplus before the market falls.'

'Lambs, too?'

'Some. He might have to make a few tough decisions.'

This was a dismal conversation and she couldn't contribute. Nick hadn't said anything about university and she was dying to ask. She watched as he lit a cigarette. 'How's uni going?' she tried.

'Uni's great.' He turned to smile at her. 'I'm so lucky to be there.'

'What's the best part, do you think?'

'Probably drawing and modelling, and we study the relationships of people to their environments... right up my alley for designing homes.'

'I remember you told me that in the kitchen at Wilga Park.'

'Really? You funny thing. What a good memory.'

Sandra held back a giggle. 'What else do you like?'

'Oh, the history and philosophy of architecture, getting ideas across, team work. But drawing is my favourite. And I knew I'd like Lloyd Rees' lectures – he's Dean of the Faculty now.'

It all sounded very grand to Sandra. Nick was quietly achieving his ambition, but there was a shadow in his face when he finished speaking.

'It's all good,' he went on, gazing into the distance as he drew on the smoke. 'It's what I always wanted, but I know Dad's feeling it. It's not just the place, his stud merinos... you know I'm the only son, and I feel the weight of it, the obligations.'

'To take over Wilga Park?'

'Be a partner with him to run the place and eventually take over. Part of me wants that too, and part of me runs like hell away from it.'

She pictured Nick as she'd first met him, dressed in polo shirt and moleskins, the white helmet, at ease with Toffee. 'Do you miss polocrosse too?' she asked

'Yes. My team mates, and old Angus. No one in Sydney knows what I'm talking about – it's all rugby. I couldn't play football even if I wanted to.'

'Your bad back—'

'Yeah, I still have to be careful.' He grinned. 'Good thing I can ride okay.'

Rummaging in her brain for something else to say, impulsively she asked, 'When's your birthday?'

'Me?' Nick laughed with surprise. 'August the twentieth.'

'That's a coincidence, mine's the twentieth of April.' Already she imagined the rack of birthday cards, the fun of choosing one.

Nick stubbed his cigarette on the log. 'Easy to remember the date,' he said. 'Come on, we'd better get going. It'll take a good hour to ride home.'

Home, Sandra thought – home to Wilga Park. And at last she'd found out the date of Nick's birthday. It felt so magical. Indeed, the entire day was magical. Here she was, riding on horseback with Nick, not unlike her dreams where they'd ridden their ponies along mountain trails, chasing the elusive brumbies. Poking quietly along, Nick beside her on Toffee, occasionally bumping legs. She wanted to feel his hands around her waist again. His grey-green eyes... *Winter's Day* sang in her mind, riding through winter grass – not the staccato of horses' hooves but rather a quiet rustle as the horses made their way across the home paddocks, and finally to the last gate.

Again, Nick reached up to her as preparing to dismount, Sandra kicked her foot from the stirrup, swinging her leg – rather expertly, she thought – across Paddy's fat rump. Did he leave his hands there a trifle longer than necessary? Was she imagining that he stood a little closer than necessary?

'Yoohoo,' Mrs Morgan called, banging out from the back door of the kitchen. 'Oh, my old hat, it suits you. Did you like riding Paddy, dear? I remember my first ride I couldn't sit down for a week. Nick looked after you though, didn't you Nick? Not like your father who had me on the horse all day long.'

'It was lovely. Paddy's a dear old horse, and I wasn't scared for even a second.'

'Sandra did really well.' Nick rested their saddles on the pole fence. 'She's a natural.'

He handed her a brush and together they gave both horses a rub down then let them go in a yard with an armful of hay. Sandra ran her hand down Paddy's neck, patting his thick winter coat to say goodbye.

'Not much water in the creek,' Nick remarked to his mother. 'Dad will have to keep an eye on it from now on. The creek, and the windmill in the top paddock.'

'Your father's been through more than one dry spell,' Mrs Morgan said. 'All the same, he misses you, Nick.'

'I know, Mum.' He put the brushes and bridles with the saddles. 'He reminds me every morning we take the truck out to feed the ewes.'

'He's proud of you, all the same,' Mrs Morgan said. 'Now, come inside and have your lunch. We've already eaten.'

In the late afternoon, everyone gathered on the northern veranda, screened against summer mosquitoes. A hedge of rosemary bushes grew along the garden fence, and beyond, a line of peppertrees.

'Nick tells me you gave him a song you've written?' Mrs Morgan left the question suspended. 'Are you going to play it for us?'

'Today?' Sandra asked, unexpectedly nervous.

Harry Morgan emerged from his office, and putting his empty mug on the veranda table, he said, 'By jove, a song. We'd better hear that.'

'I might get back to the Ferrari's a bit too late—'

'Nick was going to run you in, but why not stay the night with us?' Mrs Morgan offered.

'Golly...' Sandra said, confused and surprised at the invitation. She badly wanted to accept, but what about Emilia? They'd be expecting her – dinner would be ready soon, Nonna busy in the kitchen...

'I'll phone Mrs Ferrari,' Mrs Morgan said. 'We know each other very well these days – we buy all our vegetables from their shop, and very good they are too. I'm sure she'll understand. And you can phone your father to tell him you're here with us.'

It was too good to refuse. 'Thank you, I'd like to stay,' Sandra said, mentally reeling. *Like to stay... I'd LOVE to stay.*

'The telephone's in the study,' Mrs Morgan said. 'Turn the handle several times to ring the exchange, and when you give the number you'll be connected.'

Nothing had changed in the homestead. Her feet cushioned by the thick carpet, Sandra followed Mrs Morgan along the lamp-lit hallway, past the whiskery grandfather portraits in their gilded frames, past several bedroom doors.

'Here's the guest room. The bed's all made up and you'll find extra blankets in the cupboard if you're cold. Your own bathroom is the next door along, and we always have extra toothbrushes for unexpected guests.'

'Thank you, it's beautiful.'

After Mrs Morgan had gone, Sandra carefully inspected the room. A watercolour painting hung above the double bed, and the wardrobe and dressing table gleamed with polish. She quietly slid open a drawer: empty, neatly lined with flowered paper. A cheval mirror stood in a corner, angled towards the room. Sitting on the high bed, she bounced gently. A fat eiderdown lay folded on the end. This was a very comfy bed. Yes, she would sleep very well in this bed.

French doors opened to the veranda and through the glass she saw Nick and his father by the garden gate. Mr Morgan looked very serious and so did Nick. She remembered the blazing row she'd overheard when her family first visited Wilga Park. Harry Morgan had thundered to Nick about inheriting the property, and Nick steadfastly refused.

Pulling across the curtains, she left the doors open a crack. Tonight she would sleep beneath the eiderdown in the big warm bed, feel the breath of the bush on her face, all the scents of the night.

She inspected the bathroom, rinsed her face in the basin, combing tangles from her hair. Wish I had a dress to wear, she thought. Packed in the bottom of her bag with her navy slacks was another sweater, lighter wool in case it wasn't so cold, and thankfully she pulled it on, pleased with the effect of aqua angora against her fair skin.

A knock on the door, and Mrs Morgan said, 'This is one of mine,' holding out a long white nightgown. 'It might be rather large for you, but you'll be cosy.' She laid the nightgown on the pillow. 'It's lovely to have you here, dear. Another girl in the house! And when you're ready, we'd like to hear your recital.'

As if it's a program, Sandra thought, finding her way to the lounge room. Nick and Harry each sat in an armchair by a quiet fire, apparently done with talking.

'Enough to take the chill off the air,' Mr Morgan said, shifting the logs with a poker. 'Old sandalwood makes a good fire.' He poured another beer for himself and Nick, a shandy for Mrs Morgan, and lemonade for Sandra. She hesitated to say she was eighteen and old enough…

'Are you ready to entertain us?' Nick beckoned, and she followed him to the study, to the tall upright piano she remembered so well. At the long-ago party, the guests had insisted she play, and she was so nervous it was almost impossible.

Not now though. No longer that shy fourteen-year old girl, she felt a new confidence here in the company of people who had already heard her play at the Curradeen concert. She ran her fingers lightly over the keys, saw that Nick's parents were seated together on the couch, faces expectant.

Nick stayed by the piano as she began *Clair de Lune*. Reflections in the rosewood panels: her face and Nick's… she felt the rhythmic tap of his fingers on the stool… *andante tres expressif.* So many times he'd stood beside her like this, so many times she'd seen him reflected in her piano at home, turning the pages… echo of her dreams. Until Mister L'estrange. Biting her lip, she fumbled the final bars, corrected, tried to end with a flourish.

'Gosh I'm sorry, I made a mess of it,' she said, cross with herself. It had been perfect for Miss Brooks.

'It's a very difficult piece,' Mrs Morgan consoled her. 'I never could play it properly, try as I might. Well now, what about Nick's song?'

'It's called *Winter's Day.*' Sandra focussed straight ahead, determined not to look at Nick. Concentrate, she told herself – her own composition played a million times both in her head and on the piano...

Breathing a count of three and lifting her wrists to begin, she pictured their ride that morning: *andante con brio* as they ambled towards the creek on a blue-sky day, then a change in beat *allegretto* for the staccato stamp of horses' hooves on frosty ground. It was working – the room was charged with silence. The melody progressed until finally she played the cadence... *largo,* for the peace of evening, the way she saw shadows lengthening across the paddocks as they sat in their veranda chairs that afternoon.

No one spoke as Sandra finished her piece. Wondering at the silence, she turned to the Morgans. Nick's mother was wiping a tear from her cheek. Harry Morgan sat, motionless.

Nick put his hand on her shoulder. 'That's the best thing,' he said, 'that anyone ever gave me.'

As she looked up at him to see his face, Nick leaned down to kiss her, once more lightly touching his lips to her forehead.

'My dear Sandra,' Mrs Morgan said. 'How do you find such a beautiful song in your own dear little head? I can hardly believe it.'

'By jove,' Mr Morgan said, collecting himself. 'That was top class. I liked it better than the first one. Now, play it once more, please, before we have dinner. I think we'll open a special bottle of wine, Beth, what do you say? Celebrate a new talent?'

Mrs Morgan set the dining table with a cloth and silver; two candles burned in the centre, with a bowl of pink winter roses; a water jug and glasses. Everything was neat and correct, like Mrs

Morgan herself, in her straight wool skirt and blouse, her pearl necklace and rings.

'I've cooked a roast,' she said. 'Nick says he misses my roast dinners, so here we are.'

Mr Morgan stood to carve, waving the knife: 'You'll never see a leg this size in your city butchers. Saltbush-fed, two-year old wether. Best meat in the world.'

'Harry's right,' Mrs Morgan said, 'and you'd pay a fortune, if you could find it.'

Nick raised his glass of wine, giving Sandra a wink. 'I'm going to propose a toast,' he said. 'To Sandra: Australia's most promising young composer.'

Three glasses were raised and Sandra felt a flush deepen, beginning at her chest and warming all the way to her hairline. The wine was a ruby in her glass – no question of her age now – and she took up her glass to join in. This visit was turning into the most marvellous occasion.

After dinner, they gathered in the lounge room and Mr Morgan turned on the TV to watch the news.

'Regular as clockwork,' Nick said. 'Dad will never do without knowing what's happening in the world. And naturally, the weather report is sacred.'

Harry Morgan stretched out his legs, lit a cigarette and passed the pack to Nick. Covertly, Sandra cast a glance around the room. On the sideboard stood several family photos framed in silver: a new photo of Nick in the centre of the group, his arm around the neck of his horse. A lamp in the corner of the room illuminated Beth Morgan's contented face; and Harry, strong and confident – a cravat tucked into his shirt collar, a tweedy jacket. Sandra smiled to herself: *Lord of the manor.*

'This year seems to be getting worse and worse,' Mr Morgan declared when the news finished. 'I don't like how Australia's quietly getting involved in Vietnam.' He prodded vigorously at the fire. 'Now President Kennedy's dead and gone, we've got this Johnson cove. Who knows what'll happen.'

Sandra remained silent. She hadn't read the papers, except about the Beatles concert in Sydney. Her family didn't mention Vietnam, unless something came on TV.

'Did you know,' Mr Morgan growled, 'our government might bring back conscription for twenty-year old boys? Two years in the army, then three in the Reserves. They say it'll be like a lottery with dates on a wooden marble to pull out of a barrel. What next, I ask you!'

Nick lit another cigarette, drew on it and exhaled slowly. 'I'm too old, and I couldn't go anyway.'

'You'd be exempt with your bad back,' his mother said, adding, 'and your university studies.'

'No, I don't like it one bit,' Mr Morgan went on, as if no one had spoken. 'Menzies was too quick off the mark back in 1950, sending our troops to Korea. This is Eisenhower and his domino theory.'

Sandra wanted to say, 'I asked my father about the Korean War and how it started, because no one ever talked about it, even at school,' but she thought it better to keep quiet.

'I think it sounds very logical,' Mrs Morgan said. 'The communists might take over one Asian country after another, just like dominos.'

'It's enough we sent advisers to Vietnam in '62.' Fingering his moustache, Mr Morgan stood a moment by the fire. 'Well, I'm going to check some accounts in the office.' A smile flitted across his serious face. 'Thank you, young lady, for bringing some sunshine into our abode. That was an excellent performance.'

7

Sandra felt heady as she made her way to the guest room. Two glasses of wine, not even full ones. She found her bed covers already turned down and a posy of flowers on the dressing table.

Mrs Morgan is very sweet, she told her reflection in the bathroom mirror as she brushed her hair. In the bedroom, before slipping the nightgown over her head, she caught sight of herself in the long mirror. Meredith had once called her *lissome*. She'd liked the sound of the word, rolled it on her tongue, looked it up in the dictionary to be sure. She ran her hands down her body, satisfied with her smooth skin, one tiny mole on her stomach. Definite hips. What would it feel like to run your hands over someone else's skin... Nick's skin? What if Nick was to touch her? Putting her hands under her breasts, she pushed an uplift that made her smile. Almost a cleavage!

The nightdress was not so much too long, but wonderfully wide, made of brushed cotton, with embroidered flowers around the neck. She climbed into bed, pulling the blankets up to her chin. Sleep didn't come immediately and she revisited the day's events, starting with Paddy and Nick, his hands around her waist as he lifted her from the saddle. The way they'd sat companionably on the fallen log by the creek... *Winter's Day* at the piano. Lean. Handsome. His kiss on her forehead – that spot between her eyebrows that Prue said was called 'the third eye'.

The french doors bumped gently, swinging open in a sudden gust and she got up to close them. She needed a drink of water. No glass in her bathroom... maybe the kitchen... but the kitchen was detached from the house: down the hall and across a covered walkway. Maybe Mrs Morgan had left the jug in the dining room?

Softly, gathering the folds of the nightdress close about her, Sandra crept from the bedroom. A night-light glimmered in the hallway, showing her the way. Very quietly she went through the dining room to find ... yes, the water jug was still there. In the darkness of the room, she could see the embers of the fire glowing – she would sit in an armchair with her glass, before going back to bed.

'Ssst,' came a whisper, causing Sandra to almost yelp in fright.

'It's only me.' In his pyjamas, Nick reclined in an armchair, a glass of wine in his hand. 'You couldn't sleep either?'

Sandra sat in the opposite chair, stretching to put her feet on the brass fender. 'I got thirsty. Your kitchen's miles away.'

'In case it catches fire. Old houses in the bush were always built like that.'

For a while they didn't speak. Nick stirred the fire, wedged a log into it, watched it begin to smoulder, small yellow flames darting. In the dimness, she saw Nick's gaze flit from the top of her head, along the white length of her body, down to her feet.

Her toes felt cold and she curled her feet into the hem of Mrs Morgan's nightdress. 'Today was lovely,' she whispered. 'I had such fun. Your parents are very kind, inviting me to stay.'

'My idea,' Nick said, adding, 'We don't have to whisper, my parents' bedroom is at the other end of the house.'

So it had been Nick's idea to ask her to stay? Curiouser and curiouser.

'I knew we wouldn't get around to the piano till late – it was the only way to hear you play,' he said, spoiling Sandra's image.

The log hadn't caught fire after all, and Sandra felt the chill begin to creep around her. 'I better go back to bed.' She stood carefully, keeping the nightdress wrapped snugly, aware that she wore nothing underneath it.

'Mum's nightie,' Nick said. 'You could be a Victorian lady, you just need some flowers in your hair.'

They stood by the dying fire, and Nick put his arms around her shoulders. 'Don't get cold.'

Conscious of his breath in her hair, his warmth, her heart lurched, waiting for the kiss on her forehead.

Nick touched his lips to hers... touched again, as if to guess her feelings with a kiss. The wine, tonight's music, scent of his skin, the soft fullness of his lips... shape of his body against hers through nightie and pyjamas – the strength almost went from her legs.

'Good night, my pretty piano player,' he said into her hair. 'See you in the morning. I have to get up early to help with the feed.'

As Sandra lay in her big bed, the curtain drawn aside so she could see across the moonlit garden, she pressed a finger to her lips. My first kiss, she reflected. An unbelievable kiss. Wanted it again, because somehow, something had been missing.

A gentle tap on her door as Mrs Morgan, wrapped in a woolly dressing gown, came in bearing a tray. Sandra pushed back the eiderdown, saw it was past seven-thirty and she'd slept in.

'Good morning, dear, I've brought you a cup of tea. It's a frosty morning.' Mrs Morgan set the tray beside her. 'Nick and Harry left very early. He's worried about his prize ewes. They'll be back later, but I'll take you into town. We don't want Emilia to be wondering where you've got to.'

Mrs Morgan bustled out the door, and Sandra sat up to drink her tea, cross with herself for not waking earlier. How was it possible that Nick could go off like that? No goodbye. No, 'I'll see you in Sydney.'

Confusing thoughts assaulted her on the drive to town, Mrs Morgan chatting beside her.

Nothing but an empty kiss last night. So what was it all about?

7

Sandra found Emilia under a blanket on her bed. Emilia wasn't happy. Throwing back the blanket, she said accusingly, 'Mamma had dinner all ready and you didn't ring up till five o'clock.'

Sandra put her handbag on the bed, but Emilia pushed it away. 'Same as when you visited me last time. You didn't really come to see me, you came to see Nick.'

'It's not like that—'

'You're a selfish pig.'

Emilia refused to face her, and Sandra saw she'd been crying.

'I'm sorry, Emmy. Your mother didn't seem to mind when Mrs Morgan phoned—'

Emilia reared up, her face red with anger. She shrieked, as Sandra knew that only Emilia could shriek, 'You pretend that you want to visit me, but all the time it's Nick.' She sucked in a deep breath, 'And you're a sneak too, because I know you still like your old piano teacher, and you say you like Nick, but it's not possible to like two people at the same time – not like that.'

Mrs Ferrari appeared in the doorway, her usually sunny face crestfallen. 'Is no good,' she said. 'Best friends fighting again. What is it this time?'

'Emmy's cross because I stayed at Morgans' last night—' Sandra blurted.

'*Sì*, Emilia, I know you are unhappy Sandra stayed with Morgans. But Nick is an important friend too.'

'But Mamma, why does she pretend?' Emilia asked, blowing her nose on a handkerchief.

'She stay only one day with Morgans. Three more days with us. No more cross, *per favore*.'

Emilia heaved a great sigh. Reluctantly she put her arms around Sandra, kissed her on each cheek. 'I'm sorry, I'm a selfish pig too,' she said, not looking at her.

♪

five.

The corner of an envelope poked out of the letterbox – Emilia's awkward handwriting: **Miss Sandra Abbott**. Sandra had just arrived home from her disastrous visit to Emilia, so why was she writing so soon – why write at all?

Sandra tore it open. The envelope was lined with green tissue, violet ink on tissue pages. What, now Emilia was writing to her on tissue paper? It looked expensive, the paper was fine. Show-off, Sandra thought, wondering why Emilia would choose it. Unfolding the letter, she sat at her desk to read it.

> "Ferrari's Farm", Curradeen.
> 12 June, 1964.
>
> Dear Sandra,
>
> I wanted to write to you to make sure everything is all right because we had such a fight and I don't want it to be like that. Mamma is right, we are best friends and I think maybe your jealous because now I live with Nick's grandparents when I'm at college and you don't like it.
>
> I know you still like Mister L'estrange, because I saw how you looked at him at your Auntie's party. Mr. L is very handsome and I think he is exotic and this is maybe why you like him?
>
> I want you to know that <u>I like Nick very much</u> and I know for sure he likes me too. I always see him when he's on holidays because I'm on holidays too, and twice he came to stay with his grandma and pa and I never told you.

If you say you still like Nick I will back off, but I like him a lot. Please write and tell me what you think.

With love from
Emilia xox

It was all Sandra could do not to scream angrily at Emilia, screw up the letter and hurl it across the room. How dare Emilia write such hateful words! She kept it a secret and so did Nick. Sandra had such a beautiful day with Nick, but if there was something going on with Emilia, why did he kiss her, standing so close and Sandra in her nightie so he would've felt *everything* through the nightdress. How dare he do that!

She read it again, desperately wondering why Emilia, her Emmy, had never told her. She was a coward, that was it. So much for their promises: *Remember our pact to be friends forever?* She wouldn't answer the letter. Or if she did, what could she say? Yes, I like Nick, of course I like Nick, more than ever.

But love? Really, Sandra didn't know. She'd waited so long, so very long. Perhaps Emilia was right, and she loved both men. One was unattainable and the other...

Sandra waited for the bus, Emilia's letter crumpled in her pocket. Please let auntie be home by herself, she told whoever or whatever might be listening to her thoughts. Not Mister L'estrange, please.

Once upon a time she would've run to see Aunt Meredith without a second thought – the one person who seemed to understand her. No judgement, offering only her advice and support. Dear Meredith, who also had confided in Sandra, spilling the story of her lost love, William. She would understand this situation too, just as she understood it when Sandra ran away after arguments with her parents about school.

It was already cold, although it couldn't be much past midday. Sandra knew that Mister L'estrange often went out by himself on a Sunday. He liked to join his musician friends to play new pieces at one of the jazz clubs. Meredith occasionally joined him, but today... it was a calculated guess she would be at home, and if not... well, Sandra would get the bus home.

Meredith's car was in the driveway. No sign of his car. The front door was closed, but she could see a light in the lounge room. So far, so good.

Opening the door to her knock, Meredith swept Sandra inside with a hug and a kiss. 'Sandra, how lovely to see you. What's been keeping you away?'

'Oh Auntie, something awful's happened,' Sandra began.

'Nothing so awful that I wouldn't have had your mother on the phone already,' Meredith gave a little laugh. 'Sit down and tell me all about it. Is it a love affair? What about Nick, I know you and Donald went back to Curradeen—'

'Yes, and that's the problem.' She couldn't hold back her tears – tears that anger had checked when she read Emilia's hateful words. 'I got this letter,' she snuffled, dropping the envelope in Meredith's lap.

Carefully Meredith took out the pages, raising her eyebrows at the flimsy pale green, the violet ink. 'Very dramatic,' she said, and then was silent as she read the brief letter.

'Dear me, no wonder you're upset. Did you have any idea?'

'No, never. She never said anything and neither did Nick.'

'I'll make us a cuppa, back in a minute—'

'Is Mister L'estrange out?'

'Eric's around somewhere, not far away.'

This brought on a new burst of weeping. He was the last person Sandra would ever want to see right now.

Meredith returned with two mugs of tea and they sat together on the couch. 'You know,' she said, 'this could all be one-sided. Emilia's wishful thinking?'

'It's true, Auntie, I know it's true because she wouldn't make that up. Why didn't she tell me? She's a mean pig, and I never want to see her again.'

'But Angela said you had a wonderful day at Wilga Park. Nick took you on a ride, and you unexpectedly stayed the night. Surely that shows you something?'

Sandra couldn't speak for the ache of tears in her throat, her runny nose. She wiped it away and put her head on Meredith's lap, squashing the letter. Taking a deep breath, she sighed, long and heavy. 'Nick kissed me,' she admitted.

'Aah, then perhaps you have nothing to worry about.'

'No, Auntie. Emilia boards with his grandparents in Melbourne. Plus she'll see him every single holiday. I hardly ever get to see him even when he's at uni.'

'Sandra, darling, there's nothing you can do. You need to let this work out the way it will. Remember I told you when you first moved to Randwick: life is full of variables, and all our paths criss-cross in different ways?'

Sandra gave a weak smile, 'Yes. I'm still trying to work it out.'

'*Que sera, sera,* as the song goes – whatever will be, will be.'

The front door clicked as a key turned. Eric tossed his jacket on the back of a chair, gave Meredith a little kiss on each cheek.

'Hello, stranger,' he said to Sandra, then realizing that she was in tears, he left the room, murmuring, 'I've got a few things to do.'

'He'd make a fine diplomat,' Meredith said. 'Will you be all right to go home soon? I'll drive you – it's far too chilly to be out.'

It was almost dark when Meredith parked the car at Sandra's gate, and leaned across to give her a hug. 'Love is a heart-ache, sometimes. The best idea is to push on with your music and let Nick come to you, if that's what will happen. Okay?'

Sandra nodded for the truth of it, although it didn't lessen the hurt. 'Should I write to Emilia?' she asked. 'I don't really want to.'

'I'll leave that to you. Off you go now, and get stuck into your compositions. Have faith in yourself, darling girl.'

Meredith was right, there was nothing she could do. *Que sera, sera.* If Emilia and Nick want to be together, their paths have crossed, just like Auntie said. If somehow she could transfer her feelings into music, Sandra knew she would feel better – to write the long-promised song might help – get her anger out in the open, onto the score sheet, let it boil over there.

She'd always imagined her *Song for Emilia* would quietly develop, and one day she would sit at her piano or the desk, take a blank music sheet, and begin the first sweet bars.

It did not begin like that.

Still so shocked by the letter, when she took up her pencil, only angry notes emerged. She couldn't even think of a key. B major, G minor?

Deciding to begin with C minor, she drew a time signature then scribbled over it. So much rage and jealousy churned inside her, no wonder she had bad dreams. All her love for Nick had fallen on dry ground – ground baked hard by drought. In-between stood Emilia, best friend since fourth class, and now...a hateful and odious *witch*.

Start with the first bars of the introduction, *adagio non troppo*. Chewing the end of her pencil, she imagined the notes C, E flat and G. Continue *mezzo forte* with expression. She drew a progression of chords, loud in her head, dominating. Page after page lay screwed up in the wastepaper basket or strewn across the floor.

Seated at the piano, pencil behind her ear, Sandra placed her score on the keyboard shelf. Playing the melodic treble line, she repeated it an octave higher with a rush of semi-quavers, wanting the melody to float above the strong bass line and continue into the chorus *leggierissimo*...Oh, no no no! She hammered the keys with her fist. It shouldn't sound like that! It's got to be filled with fury – *appassionato, furioso* – except, she knew that wasn't at all like Emilia – it sounded more like herself right now. Emilia's always cheerful and affectionate, and she often makes me laugh, even if sometimes she's naughty and annoying. Emilia's beautiful.

Her throat tightened, tears prickled her eyes. My music's lying, she decided, scribbling hard over the score, breaking her pencil in half. Perhaps it was impossible to compose anything for Emilia? Grounded in anger, her piece wasn't going to work.

Angela came to see what was happening; arms folded, she looked cross. 'All this noise, what on earth are you doing?'

'I'm trying to work on a song—'

'More like the Battle of Britain. For heaven's sake, the poor piano.'

'It's supposed to be the song for Emilia, remember I told you—'

'Emilia's song?' Angela's face relaxed into a laugh. 'But it sounds so angry, and the treble is piercing. It's very disturbing music – if you can call it music. I really don't know what's got into you lately. You're out all day at the Conservatorium, you don't want to perform any more, and now you've suddenly decided to play at some jazz club without a word to your father or me.' She sighed, long and exasperated. 'We had such plans for you—'

'Yes you did, and so did I. But it's different now. Billy's friend at the club got us an audition and they liked us—'

'This Billy person, we've never met him—'

'There's lots of people I know that you've never met. I told you, he's in my year—'

'Well, right now, play a little quieter please. I can't stand that racket.'

She heard her mother mumbling crossly as she left the room: 'You faffle around on the piano or in your room, I don't know what good comes out of it—'

Squeezing her eyes shut to stop the tears, and remembering Auntie' advice, Sandra shouted at her mother's retreating back, 'Have a bit of faith in me, Mum!'

Silent, hands in her lap, she stared at the keys. Maybe her mother was right, and it was awful – a collection of notes storming along, going nowhere.

Prue appeared unexpectedly at the door. 'That was good. I liked those big booming bits. It was exciting. Play it again?'

Her *sister* liked it? What a surprise. Anguish lodged in her diaphragm, with an effort Sandra collected herself to play the piece again: so loud and angry to begin, it grew tender with the flowing chords. Following the leggierissimo melody that she'd instantly hated, but that fitted the song, the notes came defiantly as her hands reached the final sweetest chord.

The broken pencil and score sheet had dropped to the floor but she retrieved them, and commenced to write: a frame she could build on, like a garden, or a house – developing bit by bit over time until the song was completed.

Only one thing left to do...

Scrawled in Emilia's awkward handwriting: 17th December, 1960, the first letter...'I miss you too, its not the same now your gone' she'd written. Ever since, Sandra had saved the increasing number of letters in a shoebox, tenderly placing it in the wardrobe drawer.

With grim satisfaction, she opened each envelope, shaking out pages, ripping each one to pieces. Random words lay about on scraps of paper, and she took special pleasure in tearing apart the last green tissues. Finally, she snatched up the china angel from her dressing table. 'My angel will look after you,' Emilia had said. Not any more it won't!

A glance through the window that no one was in the garden, Sandra took a box of matches from the kitchen drawer. Her father burned the rubbish every few weeks, and shoving aside the heavy lid of the incinerator, she found a big heap of newspapers and cardboard. Excellent – it would make a very nice fire and she'd be rid of Emilia's letters, now all so meaningless.

She lit twists of paper like her father did, but the breeze blew out each struggling flame, until eventually one caught fire and she poked it down into the papery nest, giving the angel an extra prod with the poker.

With an unexpected *whoosh*, the ferocity of the blaze alarmed her and she jumped back. A roaring noise came from deep inside the incinerator and burning fragments of paper spiralled skywards, drifting into the neighbour's trees and scattering on the lawn like so much black snow. If she could replace the lid of the incinerator, calm the fire … but a gust of wind pushed the flames in wild directions, embers blowing into her hair, her sweater. Horrified at how the fire began to lick at the paling fence, using the poker she tried again to lever the lid onto the incinerator but only succeeded in knocking it onto the grass.

'Sandy! What on earth—' Don's voice startled her and she swivelled around, catching a shower from the hose as he dampened the flames with a strong jet of water.

'Never, never light a fire on a windy day, you should know that,' he admonished her.

'It wasn't windy when I lit it.'

He brushed off Sandra's protest, picking up the poker. 'Why didn't you leave it to me? The newspapers need to be stirred so they burn right down. It's not a job for a girl.'

'I was only burning paper—'

'I'd thrown out solvent and oily rags from the toolshed,' Don said, still annoyed. 'It's not allowed in the garbage bin, and I was going to burn them tomorrow. No wonder the fire took off. You're lucky the fence only got scorched.'

He stirred the papers with the poker, hooked something out of the smouldering fire. 'What's this thing, did you mean to burn this?'

Dropped on the grass was the angel, sooty but otherwise undamaged.

'That was careless. I'm surprised at you.' Don looked at Sandra – her sooty fingers, her wet face streaked with ash, scarlet from the heat. 'Never mind, you can probably fix it with a good scrub. Ask your mother.'

Thinking she would pick it up, Don gave the angel a little tap with the poker, but Sandra ignored it. Tears streaming, she pulled at the frizzled ends of her hair. 'I don't care. I don't want the stupid thing. I wanted to burn it.'

She turned from the hideous incinerator which had flared and crackled like a demon, and rushed into the house.

From the back fence, her father heard a door slam.

7

Ignoring her sister as she hovered at the bedroom door, Sandra ruled a fresh score sheet – she kept forgetting to buy more blanks.

Tired of waiting for her to say something, Prue wandered in to sit on the bed. When Sandra continued to ignore her, she eventually asked, 'What are you doing?'

'You can see very well, I'm busy,' Sandra replied curtly.

'Do you have to spend every weekend doing that?' Prue swung her leg, kicking the bed. 'Come with me—'

Irritated, Sandra flicked her sister's foot with a ruler. 'I have to study.'

It was true that except for their trip to The Gap, whenever Prue asked her to go somewhere, she refused. Twice, she'd given in and gone to the Stadium, but she disliked the push of screaming girls, the hard, packed benches; boys' appraising stares where she felt as if she wore no clothes.

'Do you get homework like at school?' Prue asked.

'I have to compose a trio for piano, violin and cello.'

'Ooer, is it hard?'

'It is, if you keep talking to me.'

She was stuck on the cello part, although the opening of the arrangement worked well enough in her head – the difficult part was noting it on the score – and sitting at the piano wasn't much help. Sandra bit the end of her pen, listening to the piano open the main theme in D minor... the violin would introduce the second theme fifteen bars later and—

'Why don't you just write it for a piano,' Prue persisted. 'Why do you need other instruments?'

'It's in the course. Don't you have something to do, like your own homework?'

'I've done it all. An English essay, some maths theorems. I finished quickly, because—'

The opening for the cello still wasn't right. Maybe she should leave it for a while, go out. What mad idea was Prue planning... relenting, she asked, 'Okay, what do you want to do?'

Prue's eyes shone with excitement. 'Guess what I really really want to do?'

'Stupid, how can I possibly guess?'

'Climb on the Mermaid Rock, that's what!'

'That's impossible.'

'Those uni students did it when they stole a mermaid—'

'Mum and Dad would have a fit if they found out. You'd lose your pocket money.'

Prue's face took on a sly look. 'They won't know, will they?'

Sandra felt a little thrill of excitement. Once they'd gone halfway out to the Mermaid Rock at North Bondi, walked across the first flat rocks beyond the ocean pool, carefully jumping across the gaps, mindful of splashing waves. She'd wondered what it would be like to reach the big rock, put her hands on its rough texture, gaze up at the mermaids, even climb up there somehow.

During Emilia's visit, the high tide made it impossible to get anywhere near, but why not try again? That would be something to write to Nick about. Then she remembered Emilia's letter and gritted her teeth. Maybe she needed the mermaids to finally destroy all memory of Emilia's words.

'I'll look up the newspaper to see when it's low tide, when we know it'll be safe,' Prue said.

Sandra heard the querulous edge in her sister's voice. Maybe Prue was also a little afraid. They'd seen how the waves crashed over the rock, cutting off access on a rising tide.

'Okay, tell me what day. But I'm not promising.' Already she'd decided to go – escape the crowd of ugly thoughts that suddenly besieged her. Emilia's letter. Nick's silence.

At least she'd finished the *Song for Emilia* – what did it matter if it didn't exactly fit the situation now. She picked up her pen, ruled another page of staves, beckoning the cello to enter her composition.

4

Grey clouds were blowing across the wintry afternoon sun as they stepped off the bus near Bondi Esplanade. Prue's copy of the newspaper figures stated the tide would be low enough for them to reach the huge rock. Far off the beach, two surfers bobbed in the swell, waiting for their last waves before returning home.

'We'll have to hurry,' Prue said, without waiting to see if Sandra was running along the beach too. Leaping across the easiest rocks, in no time they reached the small concrete bridge which spanned a narrow channel carved into the rock, linking the sea with the ocean pool. The tide seemed low, as Prue's numbers promised.

However, Sandra saw that the way to the mermaids wasn't as flat as it appeared from the beach. First there were large rocks they had to skirt or climb over, cracks and gutters to jump across, with foamy water overflowing numerous crevices across the platform. Far off, a wave crashed on the Mermaid Rock, sending streamers of water cascading over it like a waterfall. The seventh wave? Sandra realised she was absentmindedly counting.

Taking Prue's note from her pocket, she read the damp, smudged numbers, couldn't be sure that the tide wasn't coming in again. Prue might have got it wrong, and they should have got an earlier bus.

Like a leaky balloon, the fun suddenly drained from their adventure. Please come back, she worried, watching Prue intent on scrambling towards the rock.

'Prue!' Her shout was drowned by the rushing noise of the sea. Even the sun – already low in the sky – seemed to sympathize with her wish to return to the safety of the beach. This was a stupid idea. Stupid, stupid, stupid!

Still, she didn't want Prue to throw the old sooky baby name at her. Chewing her lip, she waited for the waves to recede then quickly crossed the final yards to the mermaids, spreading her arms across the stone, grabbing onto the surface with her fingertips. She could feel her heart as if it had seized – a sensation of thickness as it thumped against the wall of her chest.

It wasn't safe, the tide wasn't low enough.

Clinging to the rock beside her, Prue's face glowed with exhilaration. 'We made it!' she yelled. 'Give us a leg up.'

Cheek pressed hard into the rock, Sandra shook her head. 'We've got to go back.'

Prue was insistent. 'Pleeease, we're here now... I've waited for ages.'

'Five minutes then, but I'm not helping you climb up.'

In the depths of her soul, Sandra knew five minutes was too long. Each wave rolling towards the shore gathered itself to become larger as it reached the rocks.

Prue gave a shout of laughter. 'We can be the sirens like in *Jason and the Argonauts* – we'll lure sailors with our beautiful singing to crash their ship and die on the rocks.'

Prue beckoned with a graceful arm to the sailors as she sang: 'Oooh, we are so beeoootiful, come come...'

Another wave flung icy spray across Prue's face, and with a triumphant yell, *'Do what thou wilt!'* she leapt agilely back across the platform, leaving Sandra clinging to the rock alone.

Again the waves receded, but before she could take a step, another wave launched at the rock, drenching it, drenching Sandra, filling her sandshoes with water. She saw Prue's beckoning arms, saw her mouth move, the words lost on the air as her sister jumped rapidly to a high, safe ledge.

A few feet distant from the mermaids, Sandra was still not free from the foaming water which swirled around the Mermaid Rock towards her, lapping at her ankles, disguising the safest way across the platform. With the advance and retreat of the waves, she couldn't see where to put her feet and sometimes she stumbled. As the next wave pushed at her legs, unbalanced, she was knocked flat. Spitting salty mouthfuls, fearful that she would be carried into the deep, dark water, she fought the pull on her body as the sea streamed back from the rocks, dragging at her fragile grip.

Struggling against this horror, Sandra managed to stand up before the surge returned. Clouds hid the sun; hollows beneath the cliff filled with deep shadows. She knew there were stairs to the top of Ben Buckler, but in the growing darkness, where were they?

A shout came from the beach. A man's voice: 'Sandra!' Again she heard the cry, 'Sandra, wait! Hang on!'

With the last of the light behind him, she didn't immediately recognize who was calling, then suddenly Eric L'estrange was running from the beach, leaping easily across the rocks. Far behind him, Meredith ran, carrying her shoes.

'You crazy girls,' he said, knee-deep in the splashing water as he gripped Sandra's hand, lifting her sodden and tearful from the water, to the flight of stairs.

'We would've been all right,' Prue cried defensively. 'It wasn't even—'

'Thank you,' Sandra mumbled, flushed and embarrassed that his trousers were sopping wet.

Meredith arrived, puffed and upset. 'You get the silliest ideas,' she scolded. 'I bet your parents don't know you're here.'

'They think we're having dinner with our friends,' Prue's voice was defiant. 'We wanted it to be a secret, so no one would stop us. It was supposed to be fun.'

'Fun!' Meredith snorted. 'You might have thought so, but Sandra, you're eighteen; you should have more sense. Good grief!'

'I'm sorry,' Sandra said, shrivelling under Meredith's reproach, holding cold fingers to her burning cheeks. 'It wasn't my idea. And Prue got the tides wrong—' wanting to add that she would've reached the steps in another few minutes, it was only that she couldn't see where to put her feet. Oh, what was the use, she had to admit to herself – she was an idiot.

'Don't blame me,' Prue shouted. 'If you hadn't been so slow—'

Mister L'estrange allowed a little smile as he hustled them toward his car. 'At least have your next watery adventures in the summer-time, hmm?'

Sandra looked back at the rock, now entirely surrounded by the sea, the mermaids ignorant of the fiasco. Huddled in the back seat of the car, the upholstery was cold under her cold, wet jeans. Almost invisible in the dusk, the surfers carried their boards up the beach.

When Eric and Meredith deposited Sandra and Prue at the Abbotts' front door, it was past six o'clock.

'You're on your own now,' Mister L'estrange said. 'Good luck with explaining that ridiculous expedition to your parents.'

As Sandra and Prue sneaked inside, Sandra hissed, 'Pest, I wish I'd never listened to you. Don't ask me, ever again—'

Prue's door bumped shut in her face. Through her wall, Sandra heard the relentless driving bass of Duane Eddy's guitar on *Peter Gunn*, her sister's latest favourite record for whenever she was frustrated or angry.

Sandra peeled off her sloppy joe and jeans, the soaked sandshoes and socks. A raw, red blister glowed on each heel; several fingernails were torn. Was she really a sook? It was inevitable that her parents would discover what had happened to them at the Mermaid Rock. Phooey, that meant another row.

In bed that night, eyes closed, as her humiliation faded, the memory returned of how the sea washed across the rocks – she felt the tide's constant tug on her body – a body helpless and puny – and she saw herself washed like a strand of kelp onto a faraway beach. No one knew where she'd gone. No one searched for her.

Early morning sun shining through her blind was a relief.

4

The key turned in the lock with a soft click, and Sandra pushed open the door. She gazed about the empty rooms, wondering why on earth she'd offered to clean Mister L'estrange's flat after the removalists left. The last time she'd been to the flat by herself was to feed Kitty, the lost kitten. Then Irene had answered the 'Found' notices and come to claim her. 'Her name's Mimi,' Irene had said.

She remembered the confusion when Aunt Meredith received a telegram from Mister L'estrange a week before he was due back from England, to tell her he couldn't return because of family illness. Oh gosh, what a week that was – Meredith angrily bashing out notes on her piano that Sandra could hear a block away. Then all of a sudden, Mister L'estrange was back, and not only back, but spending every spare minute at Meredith's place.

Angela was mortified. For some time she went about the house muttering about pending scandal and complaining, 'It's a bad example to you girls,' but no one was listening.

After the party that Sandra secretly called *the tango party*, Mister L'estrange had continued to live in his flat, give piano lessons, and stay weekends with Meredith. But eventually the day came to make it official – if that was the right word, Sandra reflected – when he would move to Meredith's home, together with all his belongings.

The Beatles sang *All My Loving*, the big piano was hauled from his flat over the balcony railing and trucked to Meredith's house. Sandra felt like a whirlwind had blown through her as she contemplated their future duets, remembering how she'd lain dreaming on his bed, her face in his pillow. Life was certainly quite mad!

She wandered the bare lounge room, disliking the emptiness. A space above the mantelpiece showed the mark where a painting had hung; the couch and armchairs left little dents in the carpet. And there the table had sat with his blue teapot, the cups of tea they'd shared after her lessons, until Sandra eventually abandoned him as her teacher. It was better like that – to no longer sit side by side at the piano, breathing the sweet cigarette smell that lingered on his breath, the indefinable scent he wore. *Toujours Fidèle.* She clenched her teeth. *Always Faithful.* We'll see, she muttered, knowing it was unfair.

Although now Mister L'estrange was with Aunt Meredith, it was impossible to call him *Eric,* especially *Uncle Eric* – simply ridiculous. Maybe they would marry? Meredith won't change her name, Sandra decided. She didn't change it when she married William … or perhaps they never married? Aunt Meredith still kept some secrets. What chance did they have before he went off to fight in Korea, and Meredith said he was so ill on his return, so overwhelmed by nightmares, his hands shook uncontrollably. Auntie deserved to be happy, after mourning William's death for so long.

Eric had left a broom and vacuum cleaner in the flat. He'd remonstrated with Sandra, insisting that he'd clean it himself and he'd washed the windows, cleaned stove and bathroom. All that remained was to vacuum the floors and sweep the foyer after the removalists left. Easy. And time for Sandra to rub out the images of Mister L'estrange so heavily imprinted on her mind, mixed up with Nick, and breaking her heart into tiny pieces.

A new broom sweeps clean – or something like that, she told herself, giving the floor a flick. The bull-fighter poster had left sticky-tape marks on the kitchen wall, and she rubbed it with a wet rag. Nothing left in the bathroom...memory of his damp shaving brush on her cheek, scent of the man on his towels. How could she have been so stupid, what was she thinking?

Sunshine slanted through the bare windows, and there was Meredith, standing in the doorway, a big smile on her face.

'You've done a good job,' she said, surveying the room. 'Thank you very much, it's saved Eric a lot of time with him trying to organize piano lessons at my place.'

'I didn't have to do much,' Sandra said. 'He always kept the flat nice.'

'I know you enjoyed coming here. All those cups of tea...At first, I wasn't sure, but when I realized he was such an encouragement for you, to pursue your compositions...' Her voice trailed off as she looked at Sandra, long and steady.

'Can I ask you something really personal?'

Sandra nodded, and Meredith said, 'I wonder why you always call him *Mister L'estrange,* and never *Eric*?'

Flummoxed by the unexpected question, Sandra mumbled a few words regarding teachers' names and good manners. She could hardly reveal that calling him 'Mister L'estrange' helped erase her old, mixed-up feelings.

Meredith persisted. 'Is it because once upon a time you had a crush on him. Am I right?'

Sandra bit the inside of her lip, after a moment saying, 'I was stupid, but it was ages ago and he never guessed.'

'Eric's a lovely man. It's perfectly normal for a sensitive young girl to fall for him. When you suddenly suspended lessons with him, I began to wonder—'

'I tried not to, I really did.' She tasted blood on her tongue, hating herself. 'I wanted it to be Nick,' she cried. 'But he was never here... I tried not to want anyone, not Nick, not Mister L'estrange.'

Meredith put an arm around her, gave her a squeeze. 'Darling Sandra, I did suspect, but I decided that given time it would fade...' She picked up the vacuum cleaner, 'Come on, I think we've finished here.'

For the last time, Sandra clicked shut the door of the flat. Worse and worse – her secrets thoroughly shredded. Aunt Meredith knew...

7

The plan for a flat had developed during Sandra's last year at school. It had become magnified after she passed the Leaving Certificate and farewelled Randwick Girls High School. Now she had an afternoon job in the local newsagency; and she'd soon be playing piano Friday nights at the club with Billy.

She could hear the rhythmic beat of a record through Prue's bedroom door – at least her sister was out of the way. Angela had gone to bed with a magazine. In the lounge room, Don dozed in front of the television. It would be at least half an hour before her father woke up and went to bed: time enough for Sandra to reveal the plan to her mother.

Since that dreadful experience at the Mermaid Rock, and the furious argument with her parents the next day about freedom and responsibility, the idea grew and grew: a flat of her own, to come and go as she pleased. Of course I'll take my piano with me, Sandra thought, raising her hand to knock on her mother's bedroom door. Play what I like, when I like.

At first, she gave a gentle tap. Her rehearsed words fluttered nervously in her head: Mum, what do you think about me renting a flat? Quickly, before Angela could interrupt, she would add: 'Now Mister L'estrange lives at Auntie's place, I could rent his flat. I'll find someone to share with—' At this point, her mother was sure to interrupt.

'Mum?' Sandra called. 'Can I come in for a minute?'

She heard her mother respond sleepily, 'Come in.'

Draped in a chenille bed-jacket, her hair in pins, Angela rested against several fat pillows, reading a gardening magazine.

In the instant that Sandra sat on the side of the bed, she knew what she'd planned to say was all wrong, but it was too late now. Taking a deep breath, she bolted the words: 'I want to get a flat,' she said. 'You remember Irene, when I found her kitten? She might be looking for someone to share, or if she can't—'

Startled, Angela dropped the magazine on her lap. 'You can't be serious. For a start, you have no idea of the cost—'

'Mum, just listen?' Sandra felt the tightness of tears in her throat. Mustn't cry… 'I'll earn enough at the newsagent's and I'll soon start at the club. I can give music lessons. Please? I've worked it all out.'

'No doubt,' Angela said, '—worked it all out without a word to me or your father. The answer's no, definitely not. To begin with, you're too young—'

'I'm eighteen.'

'Exactly. Now go to bed and forget this silly idea.' She picked up her magazine again, but remained glaring at Sandra until finally she got up and left the room, proudly determined not to slam the door behind her.

So much for that, she'd made a mess of it. But she *would* get a flat, she would figure it out…it simply needed better planning. Perhaps it was possible to find Irene?

♪

Six.

Talking with Billy for weeks over endless cups and glasses in the student café, Sandra revealed her desire to chuck it in. Surely all her years of tuition were enough to base her compositions on? Billy thought so too, keen to freelance with his saxophone – nights at the club would give him the chance.

Sandra was relieved to forget about the music diploma. Instead, she pushed herself to learn a new Chopin nocturne. She loved the deceptive, slow beginning, its glimmer of hope, its anguished arpeggios while the heartbreaking melody sang above.

Observing her with a critical eye, the tutor declared, 'Ha, brave girl! The young Russian, Vladimir Ashkenazy, plays it.' He chuckled, 'Monstrous hard work. You'll be stretching those hands on the bass octaves, the giant chords.'

One night as she practised the increasingly emotional piece, her mother stood stock-still at the door until the final delicate chords.

'That sends shivers up and down my spine,' Angela said. 'Why don't you choose more pieces like that, instead of all those jazzy things you play?'

'My tutor's very pleased with me,' Sandra replied stiffly. 'He doesn't mind my jazzy things, as long as I'm doing well with my studies.'

Angela sniffed at this response. 'You should never have given up performance,' she said, and huffed out of the room.

Closing the piano, Sandra groaned – her mother was back to the performance problem again. The nocturne was certainly difficult, so full of tears and desperation, she recognized the yearning within it. Perhaps Chopin had loved the *mam'selle* student he dedicated it to – the love of music between them like a silken cord.

The idea of quitting the Conservatorium still lurked in Sandra's mind – but how to phrase it to her parents? She could hear in advance the rolled-out sentences that she'd heard on her refusal to audition for the Conservatorium High School, and again, when she'd dropped piano lessons with Mister L'estrange. So what! She'd got into the Con after leaving school. But better forget wanting to get a flat for a while.

Don had told Angela about the A.Mus.A diploma, but now that Sandra had rejected the idea until she graduated, they distanced themselves from the awkward subject.

'If she wants more money, she could sit that exam and teach piano – she said so herself,' Angela remarked. 'So why does she need to play every Friday night in that awful club?'

Sandra had no answer. It wasn't an awful club…leave me alone, Mum!

Billy was playing beautifully tonight, his tenor sax smooth with the piano. Sandra scanned the club with a glance: the nearest tables where diners were finishing dinner or resting back in their chairs with a glass; the crowd at the bar; and towards the back of the room, the crush of late arrivals. Her fingers slid across the keys, nimbly picking the notes; foot giving a touch of pedal.

Well-rehearsed, they gave each other space to play, came back together again. A bit like love-making perhaps? she wondered.

'Take a break?' Billy mouthed after the piece, eyebrows raised.

Sandra nodded. Although it was a cold night, the room was overheated and very smoky. In another forty minutes they could pack up and leave.

Occasionally Sandra performed solo, enjoying her choice of music: familiar pieces among her own compositions. Most of the time, patrons had no idea how she mixed it. Most of the time, she was sure they hardly listened. She liked *My Melancholy Baby*, one of her favourites – they listened then, their talk a little muted.

Billy always got their attention. She thought that perhaps his tenor sax resonated with people's lives, their memories, teased them with possibilities. Her piano countered the passion his instrument released. The sometimes-fathomless notes lulled the audience into the false security of a familiar piece, woke them suddenly with a solid beat, taking them out of their comfortable chairs to sway and quiver on the dance floor, a little drunk already.

She reached for her glass at the end of the piano... a quick mouthful, and she didn't miss a note.

The smoky gloom, candles on each table, made it hard to focus, but Sandra always hoped she might see Nick's face among the crowd. He'd said once, Sure, I'll come one night... but never turned up. Oh well.

The owners liked what they played, didn't mind Sandra blending her own work with the well-known pieces. All she was required to do was wear a slinky dress and leave her long hair loose.

Don had been startled the first night she dressed to go out. 'Is that what you're wearing?' he'd said. 'Isn't it a bit old for you?'

'Club rules,' she'd replied, swishing out the door to the toot of Billy's car.

Seated at the piano, a glimpse of leg showing in the slit of her skirt, a glass of Pimm's or lemonade handy, set the scene. And the audience seemed to love them both: Billy in his narrow black trousers, a white shirt under his loose black jacket, a narrow tie – light blue eyes scanning the tables. Across the piano, Sandra observed how women looked at him, calling for their favourite songs. How many times had they played *Bésame Mucho*?

Late: couples dancing, some cheek to cheek. Billy is so good – a gentle *Misty*. Leaning into the keyboard, she breathed the lyrics, immersed in longing. As her fingers rippled the final notes, they finished the set, and the night was finished too.

'We did well, I think?' Sandra gathered her topcoat and bag as applause sprinkled around the room. How much did these people care, anyway: Friday night, booze, maybe a lover... the weekend. Glad to be going home now, leaving it behind, she stepped into the crisp, cold night, the relief of fresh air on her cheeks.

Billy walked beside her, still keyed up with the rush of the evening. 'Imagine if we got a spot at Chequers,' he said. 'They pay thousands.'

'You're dreaming, Billy,' she gave him an affectionate punch.

'Nothing wrong with having a dream. You can call it ambition, if you like – what you used to have.'

Stung, Sandra halted, swung around to face him. 'That's not fair. I have plans, and you know it.'

'Sorry, sorry.'

'You'd do better at El Rocco up at the Cross, not those big clubs.'

Looking for forgiveness, Billy said, 'I liked *Misty* tonight... the riffs we've worked up, how you play those side-steps in the melody.'

They walked together in silence to the corner where they habitually parted.

'I could hear you singing over the bass... I liked that too. A little behind the beat.'

'Thanks. No one's meant to hear.'

'Next time,' he said, 'can we finish with *I've Got you Under My Skin*. Played real slow?'

Sandra demurred, though she liked the suggestion. 'If we put people to sleep, they won't be buying drinks and we won't be popular with the owners.'

'I wish you'd let me drive you home—' Billy's regular question after each performance. 'You'll wait ages for a bus.'

'Thanks, I'm fine.' Nice Billy, good looking, clever. Persistent. She shrugged, tired of the familiar routine. 'See you Tuesday arvo. We can rehearse some new ones?'

'Yep, that'd be good.'

She smoothed his gingery hair, touched the tiny patch of whisker beneath his lip, aware that Billy wanted to take her back to his flat. With a quick kiss goodnight, he loped away, sax case swinging. He'd be parked down one of the back streets, Sandra knew, in inky-black Sussex Street or some badly lit alley.

Hurrying, she took a short cut up Rowe Street. Rumours abounded that the lane would be demolished, the Hotel Australia too, for some new fancy business. Sad. Where will all those arty people go for their coffee, their wine, their galleries and bookshops? Meredith's *cosmopolis,* gone for good.

There'll be some taxis around the hotel. I should tell Billy, so he won't worry so much. Maybe one night she would surprise him, accept his offer. He's a lovely man, she told herself. Nice face, generous, and I love his music. How he looks at me sometimes in particular songs – when I glance up from the keyboard, there he is – eyes half-closed, full of softness.

The question niggled: what for? She wasn't in love with Billy – to go to bed would be cold and calculated. They were fond of each other, but it was a song going nowhere, as long as Nick was somewhere out there: the check to everything, however distant.

As her tutor, Mister L'estrange had been her check against Nick for several months, making her question everything she'd ever felt. When she'd stayed that one night at Wilga Park, there remained only the one chaste kiss on her lips, leaving her in some kind of limbo.

And Billy? Music created a bond, it was true…

7

Another lazy weekend lay ahead. Last night had been good at the club. But Nick never came, and Sandra grew tired of hoping.

She crossed the road near where Mister L'estrange used to live. Odd to think he was no longer there. A musician had occupied the flat for a while. Who rents it now, she wondered.

What on earth did she want to walk past his flat for, anyway? She kept walking, taking a short cut towards the shops.

Pausing on the opposite footpath, she saw how the bushes each side of the entrance doors were neatly clipped – a kitten couldn't hide there any more. Dear little grey thing – by now Mimi would be a grown-up cat. Shading her eyes from the sun, she squinted up at the balcony, the blank windows. Blinds drawn, deserted.

A small figure was walking towards her, something familiar about it: no baggy overalls and boots like before, but unmistakeably, incredibly… Waving her arms, Sandra hurried – afraid the little figure might not see her, might vanish into the air like a sylph.

'Irene, Rene!' She slowed to a stop. 'Gosh, Irene, it's good to see you.'

Irene gave a big smile of recognition, 'How are you, Sandra? Yes, it's been a while.'

'Didn't you move house? How's Mimi, has she run away again? Are you still painting – houses, I mean?'

'Slow down,' Irene laughed. 'I got another house to share, but it's a problem watching to see that doors aren't left open. Mimi often escapes, but luckily she doesn't go far. And no, I got tired of painting houses. I went back home to Taree.'

'What was that like?'

'Ooh, you can imagine. Nothing much to do. And I couldn't cope with my brother and the backyard full of ferret cages. Sometimes he likes to let his favourite ferret out, and there was almost a disaster with Mimi.'

'Why, what happened? Ferrets look such cute little animals.'

Irene rolled her eyes telling the story. 'When ferrets bite, they don't let go, and Mimi got in the way. She's got a little scar where his ferret nipped her. I spent a fortune at the vet's. That was the last straw.'

They strolled together, until Sandra couldn't resist asking, 'What are you doing here, in my piano teacher's old street?'

'There's a flat to rent. I'm meeting the agent—'

Sandra cut her off. 'Gosh, that's probably his flat! Mister L'estrange moved in with my Aunt Meredith.'

'Your aunt! Keeping the flat in the family then?'

'He rents it out. What number is the advertisement?'

'Oh look, the agent's there already. Come with me? Be a sticky beak.'

Together they climbed the stairs to the flat. Feeling distinctly odd, Sandra stopped at the open door. She longed for Irene to be the successful tenant, not sure why it mattered. 'I'd better let you talk to him by yourself,' she said. 'Go on, I'll wait downstairs.'

Standing outside in the sun, she felt relieved. Not another visit to his flat, empty, yet so full of memories. It was impossible. Let

Irene rent it, fill it with her things, with Mimi, and she would love to come. She wondered if Irene had a piano, remembered her being entranced by the old Feurich, asking if she could play.

She sat on the wall to wait. Presently Irene came downstairs, closely followed by the agent. Satisfied smiles all round, and Irene shook his hand, saying, 'I'll come to the office first thing Monday to fix up.'

'It's mine,' Irene crowed, giving a little hop. 'Imagine that, so easy. And I'm allowed get someone to share with me if I want.'

They walked to the end of the street, then Irene kissed Sandra's cheek. 'It's great to see you. I always hoped to meet up again but I never got around to it.'

'What about your boyfriend,' Sandra said. 'You told me he wanted to marry you?'

'Ha, him... no thanks! No more house painting, either. I got a job in a real estate agent's office. I think that's why it was so quick today. I'm in the business, sort of.' She was effervescent. 'I've bought a typewriter. I'm going to write articles, send stories to newspapers, magazines, everywhere.'

Irene planned to move into the flat the next weekend. As Sandra resumed her walk to the shops, she mulled over the strange afternoon: the coincidence of seeing Irene; Mister L'estrange's flat. And very, very soon, she was determined to ask Irene if she could share the flat too. There was no way her parents could stop her.

Just give it a little time, she decided, singing a tune as she reached the shops, entirely forgetful of what she'd needed to buy.

4

Over a month since Sandra returned home from Curradeen. Now it was the end of July. No word from Nick. No cheerful phone call.

She'd written a thankyou note to both Mrs Ferrari and Mrs Morgan. She didn't expect a reply from them, but Nick?

All she'd received was Emilia's stunning letter which she refused to answer. Mind your own business, she informed an imaginary Emilia.

Why should I care about Nick, she repeatedly encouraged herself. I always told Emilia I didn't want a boyfriend: I just wanted to be my own true self and discover what I could do best. A boyfriend would only get in the way, she'd vehemently insisted, always wondering *will he, won't he* about everything, like a stupid daisy chain.

Since her visit to Wilga Park, she'd gone over and over their night by the fireside. Maybe, she had almost decided, Nick just wanted to see how far she'd go? Maybe he'd done it with another girl, a girl who happily agreed? Boys did it, didn't they? Easy for them.

What invisible strings continued to draw her to Nick? It was becoming obvious he didn't want her as a girlfriend. So, Sandra decided, I will desire nothing more, either.

So why did she lie awake at night – or sleeping, dream the most awful dreams? Almost afraid to close her eyes, sensing the descent into sleep – the room darkened as the moon slipped behind heavy clouds – no light from the hallway to illuminate the dimness in her bedroom.

She saw a bridge over the river on the road to Denalbo, a concrete bridge with no sides, not like any bridge she'd seen before, and there were horses, drowned horses, just their heads, their noses held out of the rushing water, and as she looked at one, it became

Toffee, and so close by, its eyelids flickered and she cried out, God, it's still alive. She wanted to help and pulled at the rope on its neck, but its body was weighed down with debris and mud and as its eyelids flickered again, she cried, Toffee! But the horse waited patiently for the end – its lungs, its entire body to fill with water – and weeping, Sandra abandoned it and ran across the bridge, to awaken covered in sweat.

7

A large brown envelope lay on the kitchen table. Sandra's name and address printed in neat black ink.

'The card in the letterbox was marked Special Delivery,' Angela said. 'I was going to the post office, so I picked it up for you.'

'Thanks, Mum,' In Sandra's hands, the envelope was stiff like cardboard, postmarked 'Curradeen'. On the corner, a handwritten comment advised *Do Not Bend*.

'You're lucky they gave it to me,' Angela remarked. 'I had to prove I was your mother, so I'm as curious as you.'

Sandra carefully slit the envelope with a butterknife. Inside, the cardboard was covered with white paper, a note attached. Nick's handwriting...

Wilga Park, 16th July.

Dear Sandra,

She read with increasing surprise...

I'm sorry it's too late for your birthday, but I didn't know the date until your visit. You gave me your beautiful song, & I wanted to give you something in return. After you left, I drew this picture. I think you'll remember our day at the art gallery quite a while ago.

I'm still at home, Dad's not managing things very well so I thought I should stay longer to give him a hand. Hope you like it.

Yours sincerely, Nick.

She undid the protective papers. A drawing emerged: in coloured pencil, a girl seated by a creek, feet stretched towards the water, her hands resting on her lap. She wore a long white dress, with flowers around the neck – Mrs Morgan's nightie! In her hair, a scatter of paper daisies. Nick had drawn her from his memory of the night they sat by the fireside, her feet on the fender.

'What have you got, Sandy?' Angela asked. She reached across the table, and seeing the drawing, gasped with surprise. 'Good heavens, it's you.' She held it at arm's length. 'It's very good, he's captured your face exactly. I wonder where he got the idea for it... what on earth are you wearing?'

Sandra was momentarily speechless. 'Mrs Morgan—' she was about to say 'lent me a nightdress' but her mother would certainly ask how Nick happened to see her wearing a nightie, so she said, 'He made it up, I guess. There was a painting in the Art Gallery we liked.

'The way he's drawn the water at your feet is nice,' Angela said. 'Like a little pond. You look so peaceful. He's very clever, your Nick.'

My Nick? Sandra heard her mother speaking, but remained lost for words. What did it matter how Emilia felt, didn't this show that Nick regarded her as special? Surely the picture proved it. But Emilia had written 'I like Nick very much and I know for sure he likes me too'.

7

Elbows on knees, Nick sat hunched beside Sandra on the green sweep of the park. Behind them, the clock tower of Sydney University showed noon. Several ducks paddled around the pond, but he took no notice. The grass felt cold beneath her jeans.

Surprised by his phone call that morning to suggest they meet in Victoria Park, Sandra wondered what could be wrong – he was so silent. She'd written what she thought rather a formal little letter to thank him for her drawing, stumped for words to say how deeply she felt about it, the way his pencil had followed the suggested outline of her body beneath the cotton.

'Glad you liked it,' he'd said, offhandedly, stubbing out his cigarette on the grass.

She sensed he'd been pleased, but his brow was serious and she waited for him to speak.

'The thing is,' Nick said, 'It's getting very tough at home—'

'It hasn't rained?'

'Nothing. We're down to the last of the hay for the horses and feed's damned expensive now.' With a bitter laugh, he added, 'That's funny, I said *We*. In my head, I'm still at home, still worrying about the place.'

'Because it's your real home, where you grew up—'

'You know, you're about the only person I can talk to about my other life. There's people at uni who come from farms too, but somehow you've got more of a feel for it.'

Sandra thought about these words. 'Like a shared history?'

'Something like that,' Nick said. 'Understanding, I guess.'

'Will you go back?'

'You're putting thoughts into my mind. Yeah, I've been thinking about it. I talked with my tutors and I'm going to defer. I'll go back home for a few months, maybe a year. Try to sort something out for the old man.' Face clouded, he leaned back on his elbows. 'Heck, he's not that old, but this drought has aged him. That night you played my song – it's the first time I've seen Dad so happy for ages.'

She tucked his comment away like a small treasure. 'How's your mother?'

'Mum's an olympian,' Nick allowed a quick smile. 'Nothing knocks her over. She's the strongest woman who ever lifted a weight. There's nothing she can't do. This isn't the first drought, but I guess even my mother's got a breaking point.'

Mixed feelings crowded Sandra's head, remembering Emilia's letter. Why should Nick be telling her this when he had Emilia to confide in? Still, she was glad of his company, however sad he might be. He'd chosen her today. That would have to do.

'When are you leaving?'

'As soon as I can organize it. Tomorrow, maybe,' he said. 'I haven't got a choice – I can't let my parents down.'

This blissful day with the glorious clear winter sky, ducks and water hens among the waterlilies, passersby glancing at them where they lay stretched out on the lawn... so close, she could see Nick's grey-green eyes, flecks of hazel; the colours and textures of his skin. She could have pushed back his hair, kissed his face...

Cautiously, experimentally, she asked, 'Maybe I could visit Wilga Park in October, after exams?'... wondering how Emilia might fit into this picture.

'You'll always be welcome to stay. Mum really likes you.'

His mother. Wanting to lift Nick's mood, not knowing exactly how, 'Let's find a café?' she suggested.

Disregarding Sandra's question, he rolled over so that he faced her. 'You could fly. Better than the train. Save two days?'

As if it was definite she would visit, Nick went on, 'Would you stay with Ferrari's again?'

Surprised, Sandra shook her head. 'It didn't go so well last time.' Here was her chance to ask him about Emilia's letter. She could say, By the way, Emilia wrote—

Nick interrupted her thoughts. 'I got a letter from your friend Emilia,' he said.

She felt her stomach contract as if her diaphragm had pushed itself into her chest. She waited for him to speak, for the awful news that he'd chosen Emilia.

'It's odd. She wrote me this letter on paper like you wrap apples in.' Nick's eyes shone and she thought he was about to burst out laughing. 'Granny Smith apples'.

'Bit peculiar,' he continued. 'I hardly know Emilia. I see her in their shop to leave Mum's order when I'm on holidays. I don't want to be rude, but I didn't reply.'

Sandra couldn't help a giggle as relief flooded through her. 'I got a letter too. That paper's expensive.' She felt another giggle bubble to the surface. 'It's not paper for apples.'

'Well, I don't want her to write to me. So I reckon if I don't write back, she'll drop it.'

'Drop what?'

'Waffle about Melbourne, when am I coming to see my grandparents, nothing much.'

Nick rolled onto his back, hands clasped behind his head. Among the waterlilies, a bird honked. Above them, trees made lacy patterns against the sky. She was conscious of a huge lightness, an exhilaration filling her body. He was near enough to touch. If she reached out a hand…

'Ah, time I got a move on.' He stood to stretch, ran a hand through his hair.

Awkwardly, Sandra got to her feet. Another parting. Another goodbye.

'Let me know when you're going?'

'Hopefully I'll leave at sparrow twit tomorrow morning, soon as I get the okay from uni.'

That soon.

With a kiss on her forehead, Nick whispered into her hair, 'So I'm saying goodbye now.'

Sandra wandered up Broadway towards Central Station and the bus stops. If she'd dreamed for a thousand years, she never would have guessed that today could be the most promising day in her life. You could fly, he'd said... save two days. Two extra days with Nick. A little exultant skip, and she waved for her bus to stop.

What will Aunt Meredith think, she wondered, paying the fare.

'A penny for them,' the conductor grinned. 'You're looking pleased with yourself.'

7

All old houses had kitchen tables. Sandra considered that was the best part about an old house. With their plain timber surfaces worn with scratches, dents and knife cuts, old kitchen tables were comfortable for breakfast, afternoon tea and sometimes dinner; even for doing homework.

Angela had chosen a new, blue Laminex table with chrome legs – it wasn't the same as the old pine table in Meredith's kitchen, or the large, scrubbed wooden table at Wilga Park, but a kitchen table, nevertheless.

Sandra pulled her chair close to the table, opened the birthday card she'd bought for Nick. He was a Leo, so she found one with a picture of a lion. Silly, maybe, but she'd never bought a birthday card for any man except her father. *Dear Nick,* she wrote, '*Have a very happy birthday on the 20th, I'll see you soon. Best wishes from Sandra.* She wanted to write less impersonal words, but couldn't think what to say. Nothing worked. So much easier to compose a song!

With a satisfied smile, she stuck a stamp on the envelope. In a couple of months she'd be taking the plane to Curradeen. Nick had said, 'Just tell me the date.'

Oh, her suspense imagining the phone ringing, the ding-a-ling sounding down the long hallway in the homestead, Mrs Morgan calling, 'Hurry up, Nick, it's a trunk call.'

Seven.

Six weeks since Nick left Sydney, and not a word since he'd told her, 'I'm saying goodbye now' in Victoria Park. Heart thudding, her deep emotion had risen to the surface with his farewell kiss. Not a word about his birthday card. Had he changed his mind, and didn't want her to visit? Damned questions again.

With such careful management over three generations of Morgans, she was sure Wilga Park would survive the increasingly dry weather. But what about Mr Morgan? And Mrs Morgan who provided sole support until Nick went home?

Seated at her piano to tinker with a new piece, she pondered on whether Nick would ever return to Sydney. He'd completed three years of his degree. Not enough, perhaps, to be any use. She didn't know. Only that Nick didn't write, he did not ring, and she had no idea what was happening. Yes, stay in October, he'd agreed. And then, nothing.

Frustrated, she unzipped her writing case, determined to finish a letter – so many letters written and never sent, instead, burned in the back yard incinerator.

Dear Nick,
It's ages since I heard from you…cross that out, no reproach… When I hear on the news how bad the drought is I wonder how you're all getting on. I guess your father moved the sheep like you told me last year, and kept his special ones for when the seasons are good again…

How flat and awkward it sounded. Watching her pen inscribe the words, she felt the old ache in her chest, wanted to write instead: *I hate how I miss you, it's so hard. Please ring me, or write me a letter and tell me you miss me too.* But there was no point in hoping for the impossible. It was never going to happen.

Continuing, she wrote, *I'm still playing every week at the club with Billy, some classics and some of my compositions. I think you'd like*… Gosh, how did Billy get into her letter?

7

Sandra propped a page of blank sheet music on her piano. The theme was dancing tantalisingly in her head – it needed to find its place. Maybe today. No one was home, the house was hers. Prue had nagged her father into giving her bicycle back, and she'd disappeared for a ride.

'Back in the saddle,' Sandra joked. 'We'll see how long it takes before you come another cropper.'

The page kept slipping off the piano. With one hand, she held it in place, a pencil in the other. She hummed the melody, liking the tune… a key change about the twelfth bar. Needs more colour.

Billy would be pleased she'd finally begun another composition. How would he approach the piece? There's been a drought in my work lately, Sandra thought – I haven't done much of anything. We rehearse every Tuesday afternoon, play at the club Fridays. Chord progression – again the page slipped off the stand. Stop thinking about Billy, you're not writing this for him to like.

Dammit, it was always hopeless to try notation at the keyboard. If it's in your head, she told herself, sit at the desk! Her page was spoiled with crossed out bars and scribbled instructions, and she opened the drawer for another sheet. Empty. Tired of ruling her own staves, it meant a trip to Palings to buy more. The store closed at twelve on a Saturday, she'd have to hurry.

Palings Music Store was always busy – so many musicians, so many composers. Why bother adding to the sea of mediocre music, her head asked? Because I have to, she muttered crossly – it's not as if there's a choice – it's a compulsion I can't resist. Everywhere she went her head was filled with notes of some sort, questions to herself. Tutors at The Conservatorium of Music ultimately proved frustrating. The Beatles didn't go to the Royal Academy of Music, as far as she knew.

Sandra grabbed a stack of score sheets, paid and left in a hurry, hoping to catch a quick bus home. At the door she bumped into Billy.

He caught her arm as she almost lost her balance. 'You're in a rush, what's happening?'

'Billy! Oh, I ran out of blank sheets and I've got this song in my head—'

'On your way home to write it all down?' He was smiling, and she shook off his hand.

'Well, what do you think? If I don't do it straightaway, I'll lose it.'

'No you won't. I know you, once you get a bee in your bonnet—'

'Ha ha.' Her shoulders relaxed. Billy's observations were sometimes annoyingly accurate.

'Here's a thought,' he said. 'My place is closer than yours. Want to work on it with me?'

Sandra didn't answer, recalling how the thought had occurred to her while she tried to compose at the piano: how would Billy approach it?

Billy took her hesitation as an agreement. 'My car's not far. Come on.'

Sandra always imagined that Billy lived in a flat, probably rather a dive. At the Con, he always wore jeans with a shirt or sloppy joe. His home would be equally careless.

His home was a surprise. In the basement of his parents' large home in Potts Point, the entire floor was open, divided only by the thick supporting pillars of the house, painted white. To one side was a selection of armchairs, a couch, and in the other, what had to be Billy's bedroom section. Huge glass windows looked through bougainvillea and trees to the harbour.

Gazing around, she said, 'I had no idea you lived in such a beautiful place—'

He made a harrumph noise, a snort of laughter. 'Did you expect a dump? Yes, you probably did, you snob.'

'I did not,' Sandra lied. 'But this is perfect, you lucky thing. I wish I had my own place.'

'Let's have a go with your song.' He flung aside a thick cloth, uncovering a baby grand piano. Sandra spread her hands across it, amazed. Billy's parents must be worth a fortune. 'You play piano, too? You've never said—'

'You never asked, darling,' Billy said sarcastically. 'Help yourself.' He set a stool at the keyboard and slung his saxophone on his neck.

With Billy echoing her notes a beat behind, they made their way through the emerging composition. Periodically Sandra scribbled a key change, an instruction for tempo, and Billy would nod.

The afternoon dwindled into evening. They hadn't eaten lunch or stopped for tea. Billy switched on a lamp.

'That enough for today?'

'I'm really happy with it, thanks Billy.' Sandra put all the pages into her bag. 'It's late, I have to go.'

'I'll drop you home. Or I can cook us spaghetti? I make a fantastic tomato sauce.'

She was starving, even feeling a little woozy with hunger. 'That'd be good, I need to ring home though.'

While Sandra phoned her parents, in the kitchen corner, Billy chopped onions, garlic and tomatoes, set a saucepan of water to boil.

Thrilled with the score packed into her bag, Sandra knew it was early days, but the music would grow from today's work. It would develop, she would polish it, and Billy already said he loved it. She watched him – his gingery hair sticking up in unruly tufts as he stirred the frying onions, adding a fair splash of bottled tomato sauce. How fortunate to have met Billy, his sax was very sweet with her piano.

As if he felt her eyes on him, Billy said, 'You could be grating the parmesan. In the fridge, top shelf.'

Grate the parmesan? Her mother bought it in a packet – more surprises.

'Has this piece got a name?' he asked, tipping pasta into the saucepan.

'I haven't thought about it. How about *Rockin' Spaghetti Blues?*'

'Hey, I hope not!'

Seated at the table, they ate by lamplight. Billy poured wine into tumblers, and from the first glass Sandra felt her tension unwinding. The spaghetti tasted good, although it wasn't her favourite dish – winding the spaghetti around her fork, inevitably she flicked sauce onto her blouse.

After coffee, she said, 'Now I really do have to go.' When Billy opened his mouth to object, she put a finger on his lips. 'Shush, I want to go home and keep working on my song. Our song.'

'It's your song, not mine. You just bounced it off the sax.' He took her hand, held it too long, and when she tried to withdraw it, his grip tightened.

'Billy—'

'Don't go,' he said, eyes softened. 'We're perfect together. Don't you get it?'

'It's the music, nothing more.'

Billy's mouth on hers, tasting of tomato and cheese, his ragged breath. The wine, their work today, the sweetness of their regular shift at the club: always easy, always willing. It was all in his kiss, the way he held her, his mouth hungry on her face, her throat. Her head was spinning, a kaleidoscope of arguments fragmented her brain – how to resist the kiss. Billy's fingers beneath her blouse, fingers at her belt.

This wasn't the way it was meant to happen. Yes, she was fond of Billy and he cared for her, but she'd promised herself *never without an equal love*. She'd waited for Nick.

But Nick didn't want her, so —

She pushed his hands away. 'Stop it. I can't, I just can't—'

She stood up, straightened her skirt. Billy's pupils large, unfocussed. He muttered something, fixed his clothing.

'I'll take you home,' he said. 'Rehearsal Tuesday arvo, okay?'

Sandra managed a shaky laugh. 'Yes, okay. Good.'

At her front gate, she gave him a fleeting kiss, 'Thanks for dinner,' and slipped inside the front door.

In the mirror her face looked back with startled eyes. A bruise on her neck, the skin reddened from Billy's unshaven cheek. So near, so close, and she'd wanted to give in, wanted to feel his hands. A pearl button was missing from her blouse.

Opening the drawer, she took out her letter to Nick. Late October? She could go after her exams.

In the morning, leaving the unfinished letter on her desk, Sandra picked up the phone, first checking to see if Prue or her parents were around... better to make this call alone, without inquisitive ears tuned in.

In the hollow of the black receiver, Nick's familiar voice, businesslike, dispassionate: 'Hello, Nick Morgan here.'

Oh, but how it changed when he heard her name. She wished she'd called ages ago. Before last night.

'Sandra, g'day!' and laughter flowed between them, like the relief of rain.

'Yes! Just tell me the date.'

7

Through Prue's bedroom door, Sandra saw a sea of paper. Prue had pulled all the posters and photos of her favourite singers and film stars off the wall, leaving sticky-tape stains in a geometrical pattern of tiny squares. Elvis remained, and Johnny O'Keefe in his gold jacket.

A record spun on the little red and grey turntable: Mick Jagger's nasal voice, *It's All Over Now*. Inside her shoes, Sandra's toes automatically tapped to the irresistible beat.

Prue looked up. 'Ooer, you've got a love-bite,' she crowed. 'Who gave you that?'

'Mind your own business.'

'Lucky it's a little one. I bet it was that musician—'

'Shut up, why don't you.'

With a careless shrug, Prue gathered up the posters, tossed those she didn't want into the corner. 'I got sick of these. Do you want any?'

Sandra surveyed the litter with a grimace. 'No thanks.'

'I want a poster of The Rolling Stones. I can get one of their London tour from a kid at school. I love Mick Jagger.'

'I don't like his big mouth.'

'I mean the music, dummy. Anyway, I like his big mouth.' Prue ran a tongue-tip along her teeth. 'Mick's got hair like your Mister L'estrange.'

Sandra considered this for a moment. Such old history. Once upon a time to hear Prue say that would've given her heart an extra thump. 'Mister L'estrange's hair is longer, if anything.'

'I always liked his hair,' Prue said, snipping new pictures from a magazine. 'Look at this picture of Mick. Skinny legs.'

The record finished and she searched the pile for another one.

'Why didn't you go to the Beatles concert?' Sandra had been curious – her sister was so mad about going to the Stadium.

Prue glanced up at her question. 'I was going to go, but you know how you can't hear the bands—'

'It would've been exciting, just to say you'd been there.'

'I guess so, anyway, I like the Stones better. Not so love love me doooo. Plus, I didn't have any money.'

'I'd have lent you the money. I might've gone with you, except I went to Curradeen with Dad.'

Sandra flipped through Prue's records, turning them over to read the labels. 'Hey, here's *Love Me Do*. You little sneak, you do like The Beatles.'

'The other side's better, *Please Please Me*... that's really good.'

Prue put on the record and they lay on the floor to listen, tapping toes and fingers, singing a treble *pleeease me* together, laughing when it finished.

Sliding the record back in its sleeve, Prue said, 'The sound's rotten, I'm saving up for a better record player.'

'I know why you didn't have any money for the Beatles concert.' Prue looked at her sharply. 'What do you mean?'

'Because you bought that book you're hiding.'

'No I didn't, smarty pants. I borrowed it – my friend nicked it from her parents.' Prue reached under her mattress, withdrew *The Book of Lies*. She tossed it to Sandra. 'I've tried to read it but I still don't understand.' She pointed to a chapter. 'Do you know what *kappa-epsilon* and that, means, under each heading?'

Rolling her eyes at her sister, Sandra muttered the words to herself, beginning *kappa-epsilon-phi-alpha*. Each one slightly different, the meaning remained obscure. 'They're Greek letters for the alphabet, that's all I know.' She continued flicking the pages, increasingly puzzled. 'It'd take ages,' she finally said. 'You'd have to study all the references to understand anything. See how each little chapter has a note below, to explain?'

'I know *that* much.' Prue said, 'I just like some of the chapters, like *Onion Peelings* and *The Leopard and the Deer*, I can understand those. And I liked number two, *The Cry of the Hawk*, because I learned the hawk is *Horus*, the Egyptian god of the sky.'

'Those are easy.' Sandra closed the book with a snap, but not before she'd glimpsed the lines, *Behold this bleeding breast of mine Gashed with the sacramental sign*. It gave her the shivers. 'It's for grown-ups. I wouldn't bother, there's better books you can read.'

'You sound like one of my teachers,' Prue giggled. Raising her voice imperiously, she mimicked: 'Prudence! There are better books you can read!'

'Gosh, I hope I don't sound like that,' Sandra laughed. 'Play another record – have you got any more Beatles?'

After shoving the book back under her mattress, Prue sifted through her records, choosing one, reading the label, putting it down to choose another. The Beatles' *Hold me Tight* spun out into the room, and Prue lay flat on the floor, eyes shut, drumming her fingers to the beat.

Lying beside her, half-listening, Sandra pictured Horus... memory of the small brown hawks that hovered over the grasses at Wilga Park, wings imperceptibly moving, suspended above whatever prey hid far below. A sudden plummet to earth and the hawk disappeared in the grass. If she waited long enough, the hawk emerged, sailing skywards, to resume its search.

Secretly, Sandra thought the words she'd skimmed were cruel, but also musical and poetic. But she didn't want to tell Prue – better for her sister to return the book: too weird, too ritualistic, and perhaps too misleading for Prue, already so interested in her myths and legends. Let *Frater Perdurabo* stay in his grave.

Hold me Tight played again, Paul McCartney's insistent voice, and she closed her eyes to listen.

7

Sandra hadn't deferred university, as she had so often discussed together with Billy. Maybe next year she would decide: go on, or give up? Billy was quitting, not just deferring, and they would no longer see each other every day – only while they continued to play at the club and rehearse on Tuesday afternoons.

The first time they played at the club since the abortive kiss, Billy met her at the door. 'I thought you mightn't come,' he said to Sandra's astonished face.

'Why wouldn't I? We were all right at rehearsal—'

'Just saying. After the night at my place – I thought you might be sick of me, sick of the club.'

Ignoring his rueful expression, she replied, 'I love what we do. Let's not spoil it.'

Sandra had done her best to separate their rehearsal and the club from that night. Maybe he could be everything she wanted, but when he put down the saxophone and she closed the piano, what else did they have together? It wasn't something she'd ever wished to pursue.

It was a good crowd tonight, the room already smoky. The band from the first hour of the evening was packing up.

Billy put a lemonade beside the piano, and held out his closed fist. 'Give me your hand,' he said, closing her fingers over a tiny object.

Opening her hand, she found a small pearl button in her palm. Across the stage, Billy smirked, blew an experimental note on the sax.

She answered with a cheeky glissando, returning his grin.

♪

eight.

After what seemed an endless taxiing along the runway, the DC-3 rose into the sky. Sandra pressed her face to the window as far below the countryside opened out, from their sweeping arc above the ocean until the plane turned inland – the bones of mountains unfolding, then obscured by clouds until the sky suddenly cleared and they were flying above a brown landscape, roads laid out below like strings, apparently going nowhere. She was fascinated how the rivets on the wings seemed to jiggle, thin streams of oil streaking the fuselage. How old was this plane!

As they circled above Curradeen airport, among the minuscule cars, she saw Nick's ute parked by the fence. Almost there – a couple of bumps, the pilot apologising for the rough landing, due he said, to strong cross-winds. The door opened and she faced a hot blast of air, blowing from the desert.

Hint of a smile, an airy kiss, and Nick stowed her suitcase in the ute. If this was how her visit was going to be, why did she bother to come? Nick had sounded so keen on the phone, and now, here was this careful young man, as if he watched his every step.

Mrs Morgan's greeting was an improvement, a firm hug letting Sandra know without any words, that she was glad to see her.

Before dawn, Nick loaded the truck with bags of feed, and after breakfast, with Sandra beside him and his kelpie balanced in the back, they drove first to the windmills, checking the water tank and troughs. In his khaki shirt and shorts, thick socks and work boots, to Sandra, he looked the typical farmer – his lean body hardened by work, browned by the sun, an old misshapen Akubra crammed on his head.

'This hat?' he laughed, when she made fun of it. 'It's a drinking bowl for the dogs when I'm out mustering. Everyone needs a classic hat like this.'

At last, Nick sounded relaxed. She guessed it was hard for his parents, knowing he'd made an unwilling return to Wilga Park.

Mr Morgan appeared at mealtimes, otherwise he stayed cloistered in his office, or Sandra would discover him seated alone on the veranda, his unsmoked cigarette burning to ash as he gazed across the empty paddocks.

She had arranged to be away five days: Friday was her night at the club with Billy, and both the night and the money were important – even precious.

7

On the back veranda, Harry Morgan shaded his eyes from the morning glare. Already it was very hot away from the shade. The dogs were quiet in their kennels, sheltered by scrubby trees near the machinery shed. Nick had left early to feed the ewes and rams that would be saved as the breeding nucleus for a good season. Some time ago, Mr Morgan had sent two truck-loads to agistment in Victoria.

Sandra heard the screen door swing shut, and not knowing where Mrs Morgan was, she walked down the hallway, closing the back door behind her.

'Good morning, Mr Morgan—' She stopped, dismayed at the sight of a rifle in the crook of his arm.

Last night after dinner, Nick told her that his father intended to shoot some of the sheep. It was too awful to contemplate. Not so long ago, 1960 to be exact, Mr Morgan berated Nick for wanting to leave Wilga Park. 'Three generations,' she'd heard him shout, 'and you want to study some degree for an easy job in the city.' Nick had eventually left home. But when the drought got tough, he'd come back as he'd promised – shelving his own dream to help run the property. Evidently, it wasn't enough.

'Go inside, Sandra,' Mr Morgan said tersely. 'It can't be helped, I'm afraid. The dams have long since dried up. You've seen the paddocks.'

'Isn't there anything you can do?'

Harry Morgan turned to face her. 'The market's flat, they're not worth two bob. Six months ago, I put off the stockmen. I can only keep the very best sheep now.'

Without a backward glance, he strode off the veranda.

'He's very upset. This is terrible for Harry.' Mrs Morgan stood beside her as they watched the retreating figure crunch across the yellowed lawn to the garden gate, unlatch it, and disappear in his truck across the paddock. A sudden willy-willy full of dust and twigs, went spinning across the dirt road, to vanish just as suddenly.

'We should go inside, dear. Harry won't want us out here.'

In the kitchen, all doors closed against both heat and the distant sound of gun shots, Mrs Morgan poured tea. 'It breaks his heart,' she said. 'But he told Nick he needed to do the job by himself.

'You know, when Nick was a very little boy, he loved the new lambs, and once when a mother couldn't feed twins, Nick took the unwanted lamb and nursed it, fed it with bottles, let it sleep beside him, nestled in his dressing gown.'

'Was it all right?'

'Oh, eventually it died, poor little thing, we don't know why, but the mother knew, and I suppose that's why she didn't want it. Nick was so upset.

They drank their tea, uneasy with the far-off shots every few minutes, unconsciously counting. 'They get too weak to stand,' Mrs Morgan said. 'Poor things get bogged in the dams, and often the crows pick out their eyes before we find them.'

'Oh, don't tell me!'

Mrs Morgan patted Sandra's hand. 'Life in the bush can be very cruel. I've had to get used to it.' She put down her tea cup. 'Let's go and play the piano, shall we?'

They drew back the curtains, and lifting the lid of her piano stool, Mrs Morgan sorted some sheet music, a tremble in her hands. Mozart's bewigged head adorned the cover of a collection of sonatas. 'I played them ages ago, too tricky for me—'

'Oh, this one's better, the *Pathétique*, don't you think?'

'Yes, yes, whatever you like.'

'I won't be able to play it quite as fast—'

In the dim light of the lounge room, occasionally fumbling, Sandra gave herself up to the music, deliberately hitting the notes hard, her foot heavy on the pedal – anything to drown the sound of the rifle, the hideous pictures it created.

Mrs Morgan pulled an armchair close, perched on the arm beside the piano. 'I could never play the second movement,' she said, swaying gently to the quieter rhythm. 'But I loved it anyway, the singing notes, the beautiful theme.'

Eventually, after the final loud *allegro* movement of the sonata, they could no longer hear the rifle. Outside, all was silent, but Mr Morgan didn't return.

'Whatever can Harry be doing.' A frown creased Mrs Morgan's face. 'He should come in. Nick will have gone to get the bulldozer by now.'

'He might be in the shed?' Sandra suggested, imagining Harry Morgan levelling a gun at his chest. She'd heard about farmers shooting themselves when they went broke, or were broken by hardship. Nick, please hurry back.

About noon, they heard slow, dragging footsteps on the back steps. Mrs Morgan rushed to the door, flinging it open. 'Harry, I was so worried—'

Mr Morgan's face reflected the sadness of the dreadful thing he'd done. His skin was burned by the sun, his trousers smeared with blood. He propped the rifle in the corner. 'Eighty sheep less to feed,' was all he said.

On his return from burying the sheep, Nick's whole body drooped with grief, dust in his hair, his face; his eyes red-rimmed, filth on his arms and hands. Sandra had been listening for the sound of the dozer as Nick parked it by the shed – watching for him. She met him on the veranda.

'Don't,' he said, when she put a hand on his arm. 'I stink.'

She left him, and later he found her alone on the veranda. The evening air was very still, the usual daily build-up of clouds on the horizon as if a storm might come.

'You have no idea,' Nick said, dropping onto a chair. 'That has to be the worst thing I'll ever have to do.'

He put his head in his hands, consumed in misery. Looking up at her, he said, 'You know, that mightn't be the end of it.'

'You won't be going back to uni, will you?'

'No. I won't be going back. Not till this is over.'

7

After that terrible day, Sandra decided that she ought to return home a day sooner than planned. Neither Nick nor his parents would want her there after Mr Morgan shot the sheep. Nick had pushed their bodies into a gully, burned them and buried them. Another chapter had opened.

Occasionally she played the piano. Mrs Morgan always made a cup of tea for them both, and in-between pieces, they'd talk: about early days on Wilga Park, about music, sometimes about Sandra's career.

'Imagine playing at a jazz club,' Mrs Morgan said. 'You're an amazing young woman, Sandra. I could never have done that in a hundred years.'

While Nick and Mr Morgan were out in the paddocks, it was a chance for Sandra to work on a new composition. Intrigued, Mrs Morgan often peered over her shoulder, nodding as Sandra noted instructions on the score, thankful that she'd thought to bring some blank sheets.

'What about university, the Conservatorium? You'll continue, won't you?' Sandra heard the wistfulness in her question – perhaps Mrs Morgan was really asking about Nick. How would she know… he never spoke about university after that day.

In the evenings, they gathered for drinks on the veranda. No one had much conversation, gazing across the dying garden, through the peppertrees to the dry paddocks. Before dark, Sandra helped Mrs Morgan carry buckets of waste water from the kitchen sink, laundry and shower, to save her roses.

'Even the 'roos have left us,' Mrs Morgan said, with a sad smile.

After dinner Nick and his father closeted themselves in the office until late. At five o'clock next morning they'd finished breakfast and were out in the paddocks before it got too hot.

Yes, Sandra thought: she might as well leave.

'Stay another day?' Nick said, when she told him. 'Mum needs a bit of company, and she enjoys having you here.'

His mother again. She felt the house was enveloped in lethargy, not of the body – though their bodies were weary enough – but the spirit. She would stay an extra day, until Friday – by then it would become impossible to bear.

Early on the final morning, a tap on Sandra's door announced Mrs Morgan with her generous smile, carrying the customary cup of tea.

She sat on the side of the bed. 'I've enjoyed having you stay with us,' she began.

'You've been very kind, I've stayed longer than I meant to.'

'It's been good for us, for Nick.'

Good for Nick? Sandra reflected. After the last couple of days, she was pleased to be leaving. The sadness, the stubborn struggle imbedded on the Morgans' faces each morning. It was contagious, and she wanted to run far, far away from their desperation.

'You're welcome to come back, any time.' Sandra heard the hope in Mrs Morgan's voice as they hugged goodbye on the veranda. 'Just phone and let us know.'

'Thanks, Mrs Morgan, I'd like that.'

'Please call me Beth, dear. You've been the good fairy in our house.'

A silver flash in the sky for a moment, as the sun caught the fuselage, then the DC-3 was on the ground and taxiing towards the airport.

'Have you got everything?' Nick asked, unloading her suitcase from the ute. 'All your dresses, hats, feathers and high heels—'

Sandra laughed, 'Don't be silly.'

Nick put her case on the luggage cart. 'This is as far as I'm allowed to go.'

The plane parked on the airstrip – nose in the air like a grasshopper, he'd once described it. Gradually the propellers wound to a halt.

'Thank you,' Sandra said, loathing the lameness of it. 'I'll write,' she offered.

'If you want. That'd be nice.'

'Goodbye, then,' and she was walking across the hot tarmac towards the plane, his last kiss a feather on her forehead, her mouth.

Circling above Curradeen, she pressed her cheek on the window, searching for a familiar landmark. There was the new swimming pool, a blue strip in the brown. *Clair de Lune* had helped pay for that. Somewhere down there was Ferrari's Farm. She hadn't called Emilia, because what for? Towards the west, the horizon vanished in a gray haze.

Too soon the plane veered on an eastern course and the town was lost from sight.

¶

At home in her bed as Sandra slept, the dream claimed her, and she stood at the high window of an old building – a castle with crenellated walls that overlooked paddocks with sheep grazing. As she watched, floodwaters rushed in, sweeping the sheep towards the castle. A fence prevented them escaping the flood, and they swam, turning and turning – those that tried to climb the fence hung by their hind legs twisted in the wire, drowning. A voice called in her dream, 'Why doesn't someone unlock the gate?' and the water became so high that the sheep couldn't be seen, only churning brown water, and she awoke, hating it – another dream of drowning – aware the building from where she watched the flood was the Conservatorium. The voice was Nick's.

An envelope in the letterbox with Emilia's handwriting – after the last letter, why would she write again, why write at all? The same tissue writing paper, the violet ink: Sitting on the fence, Sandra read it at the letterbox.

1st November, 1964.

Dear Sandra,

    You never wrote back after I sent my letter about Nick and I don't blame you. I knew you would hate me for what I told you.

    I have thought a lot about you and me and him. We've been friends since 4th class but I only know Nick since I met him with you at polocrosse and then not much. He comes in the shop on holidays with his Mum's order and I sell him vegies.

    Nick must like you lots because you stayed with Morgans. I know because Mrs Morgan came in the shop and talked to Mamma but mostly about the weather.

    I went to mass in my holidays and made confession to Father Thomas that I told a big fib to you about Nick and me because I made it all up. I won't try to see him again because I think it is more better I am your friend.

    If that's OK with you please write and tell me.

                  love from your oldest friend
                   Emilia xxxooo

A hot anger brought tears to her eyes. *Fib* was too polite. Emilia had *lied* about Nick. She'd told big, whopping great *lies*. As for confession... that must've been hard for her, as Emilia hated going to mass, and hated confession. If her parents and especially her granny didn't make her go, Emilia would happily have skipped it, regardless of the bleeding-heart Jesus cards and saints cluttering her dressing table. Sandra remained sitting on the fence until she felt better; Emilia had been stupid, but at least she'd written to say sorry.

15/11/64.

Dear Emilia,
I got both your letters. We were best friends and your letter about your feelings for Nick made me cry, as if my own feelings didn't matter.
Now I know Nick definitely doesn't think of you that way. In October I stayed a few days at Morgans and he asked me to visit again after Christmas. There won't be enough time, so I won't get to see you.
You always hated confession but I'm pleased you made yourself go. We can be friends and write to each other again, if you want.
Love from Sandra.

The *Song for Emilia* remained stowed beneath several new compositions in the box. A striking mixture of key changes, chord inversions and choruses – the composition had absorbed so much of Sandra's energy and emotion, caused an argument with her mother, and yet... there had to be something good about it or why did she feel compelled to keep it?

Angela disliked the song intensely and never enquired about it. Prue had liked it and asked her to play it again. Her father never heard it because Angela wouldn't allow Sandra to play it while anyone was at home. Phooey to all of them.

Billy agreed to work on the piece during one rehearsal, until exasperated, he said, 'We haven't got time to fiddle today.'

Sandra was annoyed to hear her composition described as *fiddle*. And Angela had accused her of *faffle*. Honestly, did he think it was a waste of effort? Phooey to Billy, too.

Doubts assailed her every night in bed – hours when she lay awake revisiting *Song* – constructing an analysis of everything that anyone had ever said about the composition.

Suddenly, the best way to solve the dilemma burst on her like a thunderclap. Yes! She would ask Aunt Meredith to be the adjudicator.

Mister L'estrange's car was parked next to Meredith's. For once she didn't mind. In fact, that was good. Within the subtlety of his teaching, he'd acknowledged her skill in composition, supported her abandonment of the old dream to be a concert pianist, calmed Angela's objections with his persuasive arguments. Of all people, as his student, he'd given her huge encouragement.

'The decision must be yours,' he'd assured Sandra, knowing she had already made the choice.

Seated at the piano, Sandra found it all rather curious. The last time she'd played this piano, it was in Mister L'estrange's flat. Now his Feurich was in a room of its own at Meredith's. This was where he gave piano lessons now, and this was where she sat.

Meredith and Eric occupied a couch, a table in front of them with pens and paper. They waited with expectant faces and Sandra turned away, lest her old nervousness return.

She placed her pages for *Song* on the piano, regarded the scatter of notes for a moment, remembering her confused emotion when she'd first imagined the melody. She loved the darker tones of C minor – it was right for this piece.

Steadying herself, she began the introduction – slower than her original score: adagio for five bars, leading to the melody which would sing above the strong bass line. The chorus came in with a swirl of semi-quavers *allegretto furioso*... her fingers flying in a crescendo of dark, rippling chords... then a return to the melody, but leggierissimo on a higher octave. Emilia was in all of this song, in her sweet, annoying way, and Sandra knew that today she played not just for Emmy, but also for herself... a key change to repeat the chorus, her hands reaching for three quiet A Major chords to finish.

Shaking her fingers as if to loosen the joints, she turned to them, eyebrows raised, questioning.

'I was waiting for some extended drama,' Eric said. 'It's hardly *Mack the Knife*. I wanted more.'

Sandra felt aggrieved to have disappointed him. 'I wasn't trying to be dramatic. Anyway, my mother thinks *Mack the Knife's* about sharks,' she said. 'She can't listen past the first words.'

'That's beside the point. I disagree, Eric,' Meredith said. 'Your song has such tension, maybe there is indeed a shark inside it? I found the opening bars misleading, as if you're creating a trap of some kind, then the piece develops a sudden lyrical tenderness.'

Sandra played the first bars again. 'Perhaps you're right,' she said, 'but that's how I felt when I composed it.'

'And how was that,' Eric asked.

'At first I was angry—'

'Maybe you should explain why,' Meredith suggested, 'so Eric knows the roots of the song?'

'It'll sound silly. Okay. Last June when Dad and I went to Curradeen, I stayed with Emilia, and I went to have a day with Morgans—'

'Nick Morgan being the reason for Sandra's visit,' Meredith added. 'Eric doesn't know all that.'

'Well...' Sandra hesitated to begin – how much to tell, how much to keep secret from Mister L'estrange?

'Well,' she repeated, 'I had a crush on Nick since I started high school and he was a senior. After he left school I got to know him a bit, and I think we liked each other. Then, when I got older—'

'But Nick got older too?' Eric said, hiding a smile.

'Yes, but the older you get, the less a few years matter.'

As Sandra said this, she noticed quick glances between Meredith and Mister L'estrange, remembering that of course, Auntie was five years older than him.

'Emilia was furious because Morgans invited me to stay the night so that I could play the song I'd composed for Nick—'

At this point, Eric stood up, excited and laughing. 'You wrote a song for Nick, too? My god, this is all about music! I should've guessed.' He sat down again, still occasionally shaking with suppressed laughter as he scribbled a note.

Undeterred, Sandra continued: 'Emilia wrote me a letter to say she and Nick had something going on between them. And although I didn't want to believe it, and Nick had kissed me one night—'

'Aha, a kiss,' Eric nodded.

'There's more...' Sandra said. 'Emilia wrote another letter to say she made it all up and she'd confessed to the priest.'

'A priest, too,' Eric murmured, scribbling again.

'Oh, my darling,' Meredith said. 'Your song has sprung out of such marvellous passion. I think it's wonderful.'

'And so do I,' Eric agreed. 'It's a tremendous piece. But I want it to be longer. Can you build on it with variations – perhaps fifteen, twenty minutes?'

'I guess so. And I might write a part for strings, a trio.' Hardly realizing this thought had lain deep within her, she already heard the cello join with her adagio piano opening, a violin entering to carry the melody above the bass line as the song progressed.

Eric regarded her quizzically. 'A song for Emilia and for you too? Like a conversation in counterpoint, a *fugue* – the strings are the light and shade of your friend, at first in opposition, then coming together in the chorus. Bittersweet, hmm? You're full of surprises today. But no, I shouldn't be surprised, because you've always had the spirit to compose.'

He joined Sandra on the piano seat, 'Move up, and let's look at this…'

Sandra's shoulders relaxed. 'Thank you, Eric. I was so afraid you and Auntie wouldn't like it, and you'd think I was stupid composing a song like this.'

Over his shoulder, he winked at Meredith, both of them noticing that Sandra had unconsciously used his name for the first time.'

'Now,' Eric instructed. 'From the top.'

♪

nine.

Meredith dropped a bomb that no one was expecting.

She arrived by herself one evening, bearing an armful of yellow roses and a basket of Christmas presents. The family was in the lounge room to watch *Homicide*, and Don reluctantly turned off the TV.

'Ooh, Dad, I was watching that,' Prue grumbled, but her father shushed her with a warning finger. If Meredith was visiting at this comparatively late hour, it must be important. The room became charged with an expectant hush.

'We've shared Christmas together for years and years,' Meredith said. 'And this year, because my life has changed so dramatically, I've persuaded Eric that we should do something different. I do hope you won't be hurt.'

When Meredith didn't immediately continue, Don insisted, 'Come on, sis, out with it.'

'Sis!' Angela said. 'You haven't called her *Sis* for years. What's happened, Meredith?'

'We're going to stay at a guest house in Austinmer for Christmas,' Meredith blurted. 'Don't try to talk me out of it – because I know you will. But it's time to bury my ghosts, and Eric and I think that returning to Austinmer where I used to go with William, is the very best way to do it.'

'Kind of paint over the cracks?' Prue suggested, to be shushed again by her father.

'Meredith, we've had Christmas together for so many years, how can you—' Angela objected.

'Please don't. We've decided. The room's booked. We'll be gone for two weeks, and it's going to be wonderful.'

Don reached for his pipe and tobacco. 'I suppose, whatever's best for you and Eric.'

'I've brought you each a present and there's a bottle of champers and a plum pudding in the basket too, just so you don't miss me.'

'Gosh, Auntie, I love the puddings you make every year,' Sandra said. 'But it won't be the same without you.'

'Come and have Christmas drinks with us soon,' Meredith said. 'We'll fix a date.'

*

Until Meredith announced her holiday down the coast for Christmas, Sandra had scarcely recognized the huge significance of Aunt Meredith in her life. She had run to Meredith for companionship, run to her whenever she was in trouble. Christmas without Auntie was unimaginable.

Sandra knew the photograph of William no longer stood on her aunt's dressing table. So, is this what happens when someone new comes along? Like cleaning out drawers and cupboards, she imagined Meredith's new life: her letters and photos, cinema tickets; clothes lovingly stitched with happy memories; pressed flowers from a book – all hidden or thrown away.

And what about Nick? In her drawer beneath scarves and hankies, she'd kept his letter to say he'd be enrolling at university, and the letter enclosed with his drawing. Two years between letters! Nothing since her last visit.

Was she being greedy – could two people truly love each other and still be their individual selves? She'd been carving Nick's name onto her heart for so many years, wishing and wanting. While he was out of reach, almost intangible, she could get on with her work. Even when Nick lived in Sydney, he was a rarity. She'd worked hard to keep him in sight.

But Billy was right there. He helped with her compositions. Playing saxophone regularly beside her, he took a lot of her thinking time – entirely related to the music. She recalled their spaghetti dinner, his urgency. But the niggling little question remained: was their friendship more than her piano and the saxophone?

It was late, but Sandra was sure he'd be home, probably playing records, amusing himself – no more assignments from uni.

The phone continued to ring ring and ring, until a sleepy voice answered – a woman's voice.

'Billy's just popped out,' the voice said. 'Who's calling?'

Sandra put down the phone, cursing herself for being so stupid.

7

Taking a chance, on the way home from her job at the newsagency, Sandra veered into Eric's old street. Irene must be thoroughly settled into the flat by now. With no phone number, there was no way to warn Irene of her visit.

Up the familiar stairs – stairs that she'd climbed each week for more than a year. How she'd loathed Mister L'estrange in the beginning: his long, black hair and darker than dark eyes, the way he called her *Sarn-dra*, taking half a minute to drawl her name, his silver earring that had so startled her mother. *Toujours Fidèle.*

Irene opened the door almost immediately. 'Perfect timing,' she exclaimed. 'I've just made a cuppa.'

A relief to walk inside, to discover the flat was almost unrecognizable. A large batik cloth hung as a curtain over the window. Two armchairs in a corner, shawls thrown over their raggedy corners; posters and paintings stuck on the walls.

Sandra strolled about the lounge room: inspecting family photos, lifting the lid on a tiny pot, reading titles on the bookshelf; missing nothing. 'You've made it all so lovely. And the paintings?'

'A friend's work.' Irene beckoned, 'And this is my bedroom—'

Irene's room was a dazzle of colour, far from Eric's quiet blues. A floral quilt lay across the bed, another batik curtain splashed with green, brown and purple; on the floor a purple rug.

'It's wonderful!' Gazing about, Sandra sat on Irene's bed – all that remained in the room was a faint, sweet remembrance.

'I've been told all this flamboyance will keep me awake,' Irene chuckled. 'If it does, then I'll get up, light a candle and make a cup of tea. I don't care what time I go to sleep.'

'That's a nice free life,' Sandra said. 'I wish I could do that. I can't right now. But it's okay 'cause I'll be finished at the Con next year and it's easier to stay at home until then.'

A narrow shape wound its way into the room, and Irene scooped up the grey cat, nuzzling the small triangular face. 'Mimi's happy here. She likes to sit on the balcony and watch the birds.'

Sandra reached out her hands. 'Can I have a cuddle?'

While she played with Mimi, Irene made tea, carrying the tray of cups to the lounge room. No coffee table, so she put the tray on the floor. 'Tell me all your news,' she said, pouring milk and tea into each cup. 'I want to know everything.'

Sandra told her about the songs she composed and her studies at the Con, while Irene elaborated on her writing, the tedious jobs at the real estate agents, awkward tenants behind with the rent.

'I've got a piano!' Irene suddenly announced. 'Come and see.'

A faded piano sat in the same room where Eric had given lessons – that much was the same. The lid wore a crazy pattern as if it had been sunburned, and when Irene opened it, a keyboard with yellowed ivories greeted them.

'It's ancient, and obviously no one cared for it. I got it for nothing.'

'How was that?' Sandra ran her hand gently along the keys, felt the slight concave on each ivory.

'I was walking home the other day and I saw some men put it on the footpath. It looked so sad, I stopped to give it a pat, and they said, Hey, you can take it!'

'Naturally, I said yes, and they drove it here in their van and carried it upstairs. Isn't that fantastic?'

Yes, it was. Sandra sat on a box to play an arpeggio, the piano replying in a tinny treble. Given the tone, she broke into a boogie tune that had them both laughing until tears came. 'I love it,' she cried. 'No other piano could possibly sound like that – like something from a nineteenth century music hall.'

'Maybe that's it. I'll get it fixed, if the piano tuner doesn't throw a fit.'

As they drank their tea, Sandra described her nights at the club with Billy. When Irene questioned her about him, she brushed it aside.

'We play really well together, but I don't know how long he'll stay. I think he's getting restless.'

Irene told her more stories about life in Taree: the clingy ex-boyfriend, her ferret-loving brother. Expeditions to Saltwater beach, where you could swim without another soul in sight. The claustrophobia she'd felt in a small town. 'My parents live near the railway line. At night you can hear the freight trains.'

After they'd twice-drained the teapot, Sandra said goodbye. She felt satisfied that the flat was no longer where Mister L'estrange used to live. Its previous ambience had been replaced by a warm-hearted young woman called Irene.

The plan to ask about sharing the flat with her faded away. Face it, she admitted, there's no room for us both – or for two pianos. And if Billy leaves, who knows what will happen with the club.

♪

ten.

A telephone call, early enough on Sunday to wake up all the Abbotts. Don's footsteps hurrying down the hall, the muted conversation, and her father calling, 'Sandra? It's for you.'

Nick's voice distant on the line: 'Do you want to come for a visit? We've had a rotten Christmas, we could do with someone to cheer us up.'

All week, a hot wind had been blowing from the south-west, stirring dust in the paddocks where grasses no longer anchored the soil. Each afternoon, clouds built on the horizon: thunderclouds, heavy and promising, split by slashes of lightning. But each time their hopes faded as the clouds dispersed. Mrs Morgan and Sandra swept the veranda clean after breakfast, only to sweep up dust again in the evening.

Since early morning, the wind had got up stronger, whipping trees and scrub, sending the dogs into their kennels. Nick's horses in the house yard turned tail-on to the increasing dust that invaded everything.

Harry Morgan stood on the veranda, eyes searching for a positive change in the weather. 'It has to break soon,' he muttered, more to himself.

'Come on, Harry,' Mrs Morgan insisted, taking his arm. 'It's not the first dry spell you ever saw, and it won't be the last.'

'Not a drop for months,' he said, letting himself be persuaded to go inside with her.

Again the clouds built up, the fifth day in a row. Sporadic lightning flickered.

Something about this cloud was different. Seated in the lounge room after lunch, they could see it through the window.

'Is it going to rain this time?' Sandra searched their worried faces.

Mr Morgan stroked his moustache, peering at the clouds. 'I reckon it's dust. What do you think, Nick? Will we batten down the hatches?'

'I think you're right.'

'I left the chooks locked up this morning,' Mrs Morgan laughed – an anxious little sound. 'In case they got blown away.'

The cloud appeared to roll. As if drawn to the earth, it flowed and billowed, splintered by lightning. They remained at the window, enthralled, horrified.

'It's more brown than grey,' Sandra said. 'Look how dark the sky's getting.'

Suddenly Nick bolted from the room, shouting over his shoulder, 'The dogs! I've got to let the dogs go.'

For one paralysed moment, Sandra stared through the glass. Then she cried, 'I'll help you,' dashing after him, heedless of Mrs Morgan beseeching her, 'Sandra, stay inside! You don't have to—'

As Nick raced out of the house, Sandra followed the slam of the back door. A shock of hot dust hit her face like a million pinpricks, whipping her hair. She wiped her eyes. Which way? The kennels were near the machinery shed ... already the dust was blinding her. Damn it, wish I had a handkerchief, she cursed, all in a rush. Wish I wore more than a stupid shift. Too late to go back. With her hand across her face, eyes squinted, she ran towards the shed, but when she'd run twenty steps, the shed wasn't where it ought to be.

In those few minutes, darkness covered the sky as the dust cloud enveloped the house, obliterating everything.

Where was the damned shed? Hands around her mouth and trying not to cough, she shouted into the wind, the words blown away as if she'd shouted into a blanket. A flicker of lightening set her heart racing in fear.

Another few steps and she touched a corrugated iron wall. Fingers spread, she stepped close, feeling her way to where the door of the machinery shed had to be. Touched wire. Small sounds came to her: the soft, worried clucks from Mrs Morgan's chooks.

Somewhere out there muffled by the storm she heard Nick yell to the dogs, 'Here, Trix. Here girl!'

Barely able to see, Sandra tried to follow his voice. Dimly aware of bumps and scrapes on her knees, head down, she crawled to where she hoped to find the shed... falling on her face when she bumped into Nick.

'God! Sandra—' Pulling her up by the hand, doubled over, they ran. The house was invisible, but Nick knew which way for the shed. Inside, he swiftly pushed shut the door.

'What were you doing?' he panted, almost shouting. 'It's dangerous out there.'

'I got lost...' thankful tears came. 'You've got two dogs – I wanted to help.'

In the gloom of the shed, Sandra saw their refuge contained a tractor and Mr Morgan's truck, plus other indistinguishable machinery. The noise was deafening as the storm raged, and she flinched whenever something crashed into the wall.

'Loose bits of iron from the tip,' Nick said into her ear. 'Cut your head off if you're unlucky.'

'Where are the dogs?'

'They're okay. They'll get under the house.'

'Will we be safe? What about the roof?'

'Built to last. It's seen plenty of storms.'

Together they slid down the wall to the concrete floor, while the storm boomed and banged around them.

'Not sure how long we'll have to stay here,' Nick said. 'I hope the folks realize we're in the shed.'

'Your mother told me not to go, I'm sorry if it makes trouble.'

'No trouble,' Nick said. 'You're pretty brave coming out in this.'

Another long silence as time lapsed between gusts. Finally, Nick said, 'It's gone a bit quieter, we can make a run for it. Hold my hand.'

He opened the shed door and they stepped into the afternoon. But the wind blew thick and red, hiding the house behind a gauzy curtain.

Nick turned back to the shed, coughed and spat, banging shut the door behind them. Filthy with sweat and dust, Sandra wiped her face with the back of her hand, wanted a hanky to blow her nose. All of a sudden, his hands holding her shoulders, Nick kissed her swift and full on the mouth, then stepped back just as suddenly.

'God, I'm sorry. I shouldn't have—'

Without thought, Sandra rested her head on his chest, felt his hand tentatively caress her face. 'It's all right,' she said, stunned by her words. 'I don't mind.'

'That night by the fire, I didn't think you wanted—'

'I was in your mother's *nightie!*'

'Ophelia by the creek,' Nick said. 'But I'd never let you drown. Or suffocate.'

Barely able to see Nick in the half-light, heart beating hard, Sandra linked her arms around his neck. Eyes closed, she offered up her face – for the kiss on her forehead which she knew would come. *Now*, her heart said: *kiss me now or kiss me never*. Her breath a whisper.

Held in Nick's arms, she smelled his skin against her cheek, felt the tremor in his limbs as he touched his lips first to one eyelid, then the other, kissed the tip of her nose. Pressed against her, their gritty skins stuck with sweat, at last he kissed her mouth, a taste of dust, then long and sweet... and in the softness of his lips she felt herself dissolve into this kiss, the heat of his mouth, his hands holding her close.

Nick found cushions in his father's truck. In the gloom, leaning together without speaking, they sat on the concrete floor, waiting for the wind to drop. Sandra closed her eyes, re-living the moments from Nick's first hesitant touch to where she'd clung to him, swept away with emotion. She heaved a sigh and Nick gave her a quick kiss on the cheek. Confused, mystified, she could have almost laughed. More like *never...*

They discovered an eerily quiet land when Nick opened the shed door: strangely still, the air laden with its fog of dust from the inland. Several stringy belah trees lay fallen, and Mrs Morgan's old tamarisk, broken across the garden fence.

The dogs crawled from beneath the house, ran to them, tails wagging, snuffling around their feet. Nick patted their heads briefly, commanded, 'Down, down,' and the kelpies bounced away, glad to be free.

Mrs Morgan was crouched on the back veranda. A scarf across her head, face streaked with dirty tears, she rested against the wall.

In a stride, Nick leapt up the steps. 'Mum! What are you doing outside?'

'I told your father, I'm not coming in till you and Sandra are home safe.' She struggled to stand, failed, slumped down on the boards again.

Harry Morgan slammed the door behind him, his face blotched with anger. 'I had to drag your mother back to the house from the paddock—' he shouted.

'Stop it, Harry. I'm perfectly all right, as you can very well see.'

'You're not, Mum.' Nick helped her up, his arm around her, allowing her to lean on him.

'She was out searching for you.' Mr Morgan wiped his face, calmer now. 'Your mother's not young like you. We weren't spring chickens when you were born.'

'It's just a bit of dust,' Mrs Morgan answered. 'Nick, when Sandra ran after you, I was so afraid. What if we'd lost her?'

Sandra wondered at it, watching as Nick helped his mother inside, remembered on her first visit how Mrs Morgan had happily declared, 'Another girl in the house'. She realized these people were important to her: Beth, Harry Morgan – and Nick, who linked them all together.

'Look at you…' Mrs Morgan touched a strand of Sandra's hair. 'It's gone quite red.' Her voice was shaky. 'One of my shoes is out there somewhere.'

Doors and windows remained closed, and would remain shut until enough dust settled to open them again, letting in clean, dry air – until the next dust clouds inevitably blew across the country, loaded with sorrow.

Fresh from a shower, having done her best to wash her hair in a bucket, Sandra wore a new shift, her hair damp and curling down her back. She joined the family in the lounge room and Mrs Morgan poured tea. Holding their cups, they sat quietly, the only sound the whirr of a fan.

Never, Sandra reflected, do I ever want to see another dust cloud, in all my life. But if it took a dust storm for Nick to kiss me, then something was accomplished. She allowed a secret smile and catching Nick's glance, saw the same smile lift the corners of his mouth.

'Enough for now,' Mr Morgan said. 'I'll leave you all to your cups of tea.'

They watched him go, Mrs Morgan's face wearing a certain grief. 'I'll just go and see what Harry's up to,' she said, following him with her cup and saucer.

Nick emptied the pot into their cups, commenting, 'I can't drink enough, how about you?'

'Altogether, a new experience,' Sandra said, leaving her answer hanging.

'Definitely,' Nick said. 'What next?'

What next? She wanted to get out of her armchair – be finished with drinking endless cups of tea. She wanted to get moving – away from Harry Morgan who no longer had anything to say, Beth's anxious face behind her cheerfulness. The entire house was descending into gloom. The day after tomorrow, she would be catching the plane to Sydney.

She wanted to go, she wanted to stay...

An idea occurred to her. 'Remember that time we came to your place, the night of the party?'

'Yeah, I won't forget. Another drunken night with Angus—'

'And you told me back then how you wanted to be an architect?'

'Sure. I spent every spare minute drawing plans for houses. It drove my father mad.'

'Have you still got them?'

'A few, some are pretty crazy. I can show you, if you like.'

Nick led the way down the hall, past the guest room and study. 'In my bedroom,' Nick opened a door, 'if you don't mind the mess.'

Expecting what she pictured a boy's bedroom to look like, with clothes dropped on the floor and sports pennants strung along the walls, maybe a row of trophies on a shelf, Sandra was surprised at the sparseness.

Large, like all the rooms at Wilga Park, a single bed covered in a sheet was pushed near one wall. Under the window squatted a large desk, an enormous lamp beside it.

'My so-called drafting table,' Nick explained. 'Great-grandfather's desk – mahogany and heavy as lead. I got the light from a local workshop that shut down.'

Several drawings were stuck on a wall: pen and ink horses in flight. Sandra peered closely at the flaring nostrils, wind in their manes and tails, pebbles kicked up by flying hooves. Fine details, a wash of blue.

'You drew these beautiful horses?'

Nick nodded, 'Old drawings.'

'This one's new, it's got a date.' She was transfixed by the picture, the deftly wielded coloured pencils: two silhouetted figures, outline of a house on the horizon – and like boiling soup, a gigantic multicoloured cloud hung over them as the little figures scampered towards the house, pursued by the cloud.

'Our dust storm,' Nick gave a lop-sided smile. 'I drew it when you were in the shower. It's just a quick sketch.'

Deeply absorbed, Sandra continued to stare at the drawing. 'Nick, this one, all these drawings – they're awfully good! They're really beautiful.'

He shook his head and Sandra wandered to the window, orienting herself. Nick's room opened to the same veranda as the guest room, with similar french doors. There was a lowboy, a map cabinet, a bookshelf. Nick's polocrosse helmet and racquet hung on a hook behind the door. Sparse, she thought. Nothing surplus, rather like Nick.

He took a sheet of paper from a drawer of the cabinet, spread it on the desk: floor plan of a simple house, accompanied by an isometric interior drawing, and a third, realistic sketch that depicted the exterior fabric of the building, exactly how Nick imagined it. A house designed for a hot landscape, angles of the sun indicated by degrees. Exquisite in its minute detail, bending close, Sandra saw how myriad fine lines captured almost the feel of the house, its papery spirit.

'Coloured pencils again – I like the way you blend the colours.'

'Thanks. I did this one at school. I always drew the sort of house I'd like to live in. Life changes of course. One day I might design houses for cold places. For cities, perhaps.'

He slid the papers back into the cabinet. 'Now you know how I waste my time here.'

'Don't say that. It's a beautiful house, and maybe you should build it.'

She scanned the bookshelf, investigating titles: worn childhood novels, *Biggles Flies East*, and *Biggles Defies the Swastika*. Shakespeare's plays. Mountaineering and prisoner of war stories. Volumes of design: Frank Lloyd Wright; a 1950's Lloyd Rees Sketchbook; and many titles she'd never heard of. She opened a novel called *Flamingo Feather*, flipped the pages to read a few lines.

'Take it, if you like. Laurens van der Post,' Nick said. 'South Africa years ago.'

'You like adventure stories,' Sandra said. 'And your designs are adventurous too.'

'I like that for an opinion. My father never comes in here.'

Although he smiled, Sandra thought he seemed sad beneath it. The weight of Nick's heritage: a father who loathed his son's dream because it didn't reflect his own.

Thankful not to be burdened by a similar load, she pondered on Nick's complicated future.

7

A still, hot night – worse with all the windows and doors shut. Mr and Mrs Morgan had gone to their room after a dinner of cold meat and salad, followed by icecream and jelly with the usual jug of homemade custard sauce.

Nick said goodnight and disappeared. Sandra thought she heard the back door close, but no bark of a dog broke the silence.

Her bedroom was stuffy but she dared not open the doors to the veranda. She threw off the top sheet and lay spread-eagled across the bed, one foot dangling over the side for a semblance of coolness. Sleep seemed a long way off as the hours ticked by, until finally she slept.

A click of a door handle, the french doors swung open, and she woke to a whispered, 'Sandra?'

'Gosh, Nick,' was all she managed to say as he sat beside her. In the ghostly light of the room, she saw that he was fully dressed.

'It's two o'clock,' Nick said. 'I thought I'd better wake you. Mum's ill. Dad's taken her into hospital.'

'Oh. What's wrong, do you think?'

'I don't know yet. But I'll take you into town for the early flight. We can change your ticket at the airport. I'm sorry about this, Sandra.'

'Never mind ... I'm really sorry your mother's sick. And it's time I left—'

'I'd like you to stay,' Nick said. 'I'm a selfish bastard. It's difficult.' His voice cracked and he stretched his length on the bed.

Sandra shifted aside, allowing her own length to rest beside him. She felt his hand tighten on hers.

'Mum can't speak properly. Maybe it's a stroke.'

He turned to face her, his breath hot in the oppressive bedroom. 'I don't know when I'll be back in Sydney. Who knows how long I'll be stuck here. You need to get on with your music – no point hanging around any longer.'

Sandra felt the familiar thickness in her throat as tears seeped from her eyes, running into the pillow. This was Nick saying goodbye again. Nick letting her know there could be nothing more in their friendship. Hundreds of miles would remain between them. Their kisses floated above her like wraiths, to vanish quickly.

Nick wiped her wet cheek with his finger. 'Ah, my pretty piano player, my Sandra,' he whispered. 'I wish it could be different.'

He swung his feet off the bed and they stood together, staring into the bleak night.

A last kiss was all she wanted. The way he'd kissed her in the shed meant something, she'd been certain, but now...

'Kiss me goodbye here, right now, before we get to the airport?' she asked. 'Please?'

Nick's expression was hidden, but his hands gently cupped her face, held her so tenderly she felt her heart might break. Nothing comes from nothing, her head was telling her. His lips on hers, maybe for the last time. She took his hand, placed it on her heart, let his fingers slip beneath the soft cotton. So much longing. Again, the heat of his mouth, his gentle hands.

Her voice soft: No, no more.

The dogs were chained to their kennels again. At least that was normal. Mr Morgan hadn't returned by the time Nick brought his ute to the garden gate.

'You'll let me know about your mother?' Sandra's question at the airport, spoken into Nick's ear as she planted a kiss on his cheek, his own dry kiss in response.

'Sure. Have a good flight. It won't be so bumpy today.'

'I'll write—' her words melted into the hot tarmac with her lack of resolve. The old refrain: What for?

A final glimpse of the hard-baked inland before the DC-3 was winging over the green of the Blue Mountains, the red tiled roofs, tennis courts and blue swimming pools of Sydney, to land at Mascot.

⁋

Two weeks later, the letter arrived: the long-awaited word from Nick. Quickly Sandra slit open the envelope, unfolded the crisp white page, hardly daring to think what he might have written. If the news about Beth was serious, wouldn't he have telephoned?

Wilga Park.
2 February, 65.

My dear Sandra,

...That was a good start, although *Darling* would've been better...

> Finally I get to write to you as you asked. Mum had a stroke & is still in hospital. Her right side isn't much good but she can talk alright. We're very lucky it was a little stroke or I don't know what would have happened. Dad is having a bad time over it so just as well I'm here.
>
> There won't be any lambing this year. Finally the government has set up a Drought Watch, whatever that does for the farmers.
>
> Sorry you had to leave in a hurry. Good luck with everything,
>
> Yours, Nick.

If she'd tried to imagine a worse letter, she couldn't have done better than this. It was a shock that dear Beth was sick, but Nick's letter was so matter-of-fact, so impersonal, it was all she could do to walk into the house before bursting into tears. Shut in her bedroom, frustration and sorrow mixed together, to pour weeping onto her pillow.

The night that Nick came to her bedroom to talk about his mother she'd returned his affection, his kisses, and there were nights when she lay on her pillow and wished she hadn't stopped his fingers as he stroked her skin beneath the nightdress, given in to what he seemed to want. Would it have changed anything?

What's love, anyway – a figment of the imagination, she cursed. All a delusion. Safer to turn away from the edge.

The next day she wrote a crisp little note, telling herself: keep to the point, this is all about his mother.

9 February '65.

My dear Nick,

…well, that's what he wrote…

> *Thank you for writing to me about your mother, I was very sorry to read of her stroke. I wish her a very good recovery and that she will soon be back home. Please thank your father for having me to stay and especially your mother the next time you speak to her.*
>
> *I hope it's rained and you won't get another dust storm. I feel sorry for the poor animals.*

So hard to find the right words instead of dry phrases like a greeting card. She finished it with a few more trivial lines, signed it *Yours sincerely, Sandra,* and sealed the envelope. Should she have written *poor farmers*?

7

Billy had turned twenty in December and registered for the new compulsory National Service ballot. Jubilant when he missed being called up in the January ballot, he'd crushed Sandra in a hug. 'I'm not soldier material. Someone must've guessed and fixed the lottery!'

During the last of the summer holidays, Sandra's old school friend Carol had turned up, and occasionally they met to go to the beach or to the pictures. Better to sit in the dark of the cinema, because Sandra found now they'd both left school there was nothing much to talk about.

In April, at America's request Australia sent a battalion of troops to Vietnam. Already there were scattered protests against Australia being drawn into the war. Carol's brother was conscripted, and after Carol joined the *Save Our Sons* protest movement, Sandra hardly ever saw her.

At the club, she and Billy continued to play their favourites: the usual songs which always included *Winter's Day*. Billy was superlative and when his sax carried the melody in *Walk On By*, a woman seated near the stage threw a flower, which he scooped up with a grin and stuck in his hair. After the show, he kissed the woman goodnight, with a 'See you next week.'

'Who was that?' Sandra asked, as they left the club.

'No idea.' He grinned, the same grin he'd flashed at the woman with the flower. 'Are you jealous?'

For her answer, Sandra gently swiped his arm. Almost at the corner, Billy said, 'There's a couple of strangers I've seen twice now. They sit at the back and leave before we finish.'

Sandra feigned interest. The club was small enough to see many of the faces: the ones who came more than once, the regulars, the one-offs. 'Well, if you're that curious, go and say hello.'

They parted, with Sandra seeking a taxi, only recalling later, that Billy hadn't said if the strangers were men or women. Billy certainly had a following among the women. Tall, attractive, with such a cheeky smile, she was lucky to have him. On stage, she knew they looked good together. Billy continued to wear his narrow trousers and a jacket over his shirt, but Sandra occasionally switched to black slacks and a velvet top, easy and elegant.

Walk On By continued to sing in her head on the way to the taxi rank – impossible not to sing the lyrics. It made her feel like crying – better to hum it – but I'm done with crying, she told herself.

She wished she could have loved Billy, but their friendship was good, and that was better. Yes, she was lucky.

♫

eleven.

With time, the drowning dreams disappeared. Thank goodness. Sandra wondered what had caused them to vanish. Perhaps it was her nineteenth birthday last April, or perhaps only one year left to graduate, or maybe the continuing pleasure of playing at the club and composing her music. Her tutors at the Con were extremely pleased, and told her so.

Ideas for her compositions flowed from every direction. She heard music almost everywhere she looked: the swing of a dress, the hurrying footsteps; children playing in the park; sharp *agitato* as a car skidded to a halt on a corner; Billy on the sax, eyes half-closed. A man on horseback, covering the ground in an easy canter. Like taking too many photographs, she thought: after a while, you see everything through a viewfinder. Or writing a poem – when you've written the umpteenth verse, everything you write begins to rhyme.

She knew from the TV news that it was terrible out west. Crops had failed. Yet another year too dry to plant winter wheat, some farmers gave up, putting their properties on the market. Who would buy a dust bowl? Sandra wondered.

What of Wilga Park? Since Nick's letter in February about his mother, there had been nothing more, and no answer to her reply.

Sandra tried her best to be cheerful, and wrote another short letter:

10 July '65.

Dear Nick,
I guess you're still at Wilga Park. This is just a note to let you know I've read in the papers and it's on TV how dry it is out west. I hope it rains soon.
I have been wondering if your mother is home again, and how she's getting on?
My music studies are going well. Only one more year and I'm finished. I still play at the club and I love doing that because I can mix my own work with…

No good. She screwed up the note and began again, finishing with the question about his mother.

Please pass on my regards to your parents. Give the horses and Trix a pat from me.
Let me know when you come back to uni.
Yours sincerely,
Sandra.

After she'd posted the letter, she wished she'd written a better one, wished she'd said, *I miss you, and I hope you're okay. Love from Sandra*. Never mind that Nick hadn't written it first.

But he'd said, *I wish it could be different*. And it wasn't. The idyllic dream was extinguished with those few words.

She phoned once, hesitantly, but there was no answer when the exchange tried the Morgans' number. She still hadn't heard from Nick and he'd forgotten her birthday. Regardless of her deep suspicion that it was a waste of time, Sandra chose a birthday card for him. If she posted it tomorrow, it would get there by the twentieth of August.

It depicted two horses, obviously a mare and foal beneath what might be a gum tree. If nothing else, it was nostalgic. Where was

Toffee, and had Nick sold Honey? Was Mrs Morgan better, and how about Nick's father? She wrote her questions in a hurry, before she could change her mind, dropped the card in the post box on her way to rehearsal. Uni break would be a relief, before the year's final exam.

A white envelope lay on the kitchen table, addressed to Sandra. Emilia's handwriting. Wondering what she would find, Sandra slit the envelope with a butter knife.

Inside, a flowery card, with a note.

6 August, 65.

Dear Sandra,

I got your letter in November last year about going to stay with Nick after Christmas. You told me you would be <u>too busy to visit me</u> so I didn't want to write back to you, not even when Mrs Morgan got sick and came to live in Melbourne with her family. That was very sad for Nick and Mr Morgan.

Nick's granny helped me to find a nice boarding house for girls until I finish college next year. It's OK because there's only 5 girls plus me, the lady's Greek and she cooks very good dinners.

Now I know for sure you and Nick love each other. I always find out later when you've stay there and I bet you see him in Sydney too.

I think both our lives have gone very strange. Lofty and I are going together and he said it was always me he liked but I thought it was always you. That's funny, isn't it! He gets called Warwick at teachers college but in Curradeen he will always be Lofty. I am making my debut next year and Lofty is going to be my partner. I'm already planning my ball dress.

I hope you will write back to tell me what you're doing and what will Nick's father do when Nick goes back to university? You are still my best friend, whatever happens.

Love from Emilia.
XOXOX

Oh Emmy, if only you knew how seldom I ever see Nick in Sydney. Undecided about replying, Sandra knew that to answer Emilia's card was the only way to keep their fragile friendship, at the same time wondering if it was worth it. But as she wrote, the old warmth gradually returned, and she knew she could write pages and pages.

10 August, 65.

Dear Emilia,

Thank you for the pretty card, I know you like Mrs Morgan too. It was an awful thing to happen but maybe she'll be well enough to go home soon. Nick has deferred uni because he needs to help his father. I hope you'll be all right in your boarding house, at least it's all girls! You're lucky to get dinners too.

After your first letter I was so upset and angry, I wrote a song except it hasn't got words. I called it "Song for Emilia" and it started off being very "furioso" because that was how I felt, but in the end it turned into something else, and it's sort of about you and me, all our ups and downs and about our long friendship.

Aunt Meredith and Eric (I call him Eric now) really like my Song, and I play it at the club where I play piano on Friday nights (yes, I know, I'm performing!).

How are your parents and Nonna, is she still knitting? Please write and tell me more about everything and about Lofty, it's nice you're going together and so exciting you will make your debut.

Everyone is well here, write again soon.

Love from Sandra xox

She would have liked to write more about Nick, but what was there to say?

4

Meredith and Eric came to the club one evening, discreet as only Meredith knew how. Sandra didn't know they were there until she and Billy played their last number.

Meredith kissed her, declaring, 'I knew you'd be terrific, dear Sandra, and you look stunning. Midnight-blue suits you.'

Filled with surprise, Sandra introduced them, and Billy kissed Meredith's cheek, shook Eric's hand.

'Fantastic,' Eric said, enveloping Sandra in a surprising hug. 'For someone who didn't want to perform, you're brilliant.'

With a quick smile at Sandra, Billy clipped shut his sax case. 'She's wonderful – we do a good set.'

Meredith glanced from Sandra to Billy and back again, seeing the affection between them. The next band began playing, so they left to say farewell out in the street.

On the drive home to Sandra's, Meredith said, 'Billy's superb. You've worked up a great duo together.'

'He's in love with you,' Eric announced, matter-of-fact. 'It shows a mile off.'

'It's nothing,' Sandra protested. 'We've talked about it. It's only the music—'

'Maybe for you,' Meredith replied.

For a few minutes they sat in the car outside the Abbotts' house.

'Have you heard from Nick?'

Sandra ignored Meredith's question. 'Goodnight, thank you for coming tonight,' she said. Relenting, she bent to say through the window, 'You know I haven't, or I would've told you.'

Eric switched the subject, 'How about some Otis Redding? I think his music would suit you both. And come with us one night to El Rocco. Think about it.'

As they drove away, Sandra shut the gate more firmly than usual. Why does everyone care what I do? I go along calmly minding my own business, I'm doing well at the Con, I've got lots of compositions that my tutors are happy with, I enjoy performing in ensembles... will you all just leave me alone!

7

At rehearsal, Billy said, 'Otis Redding? Sure. We could do *Try a Little Tenderness.*'

'I don't like the words much.'

'Hey,' Billy said, irritated. 'We're not singing.'

'Okay, if we can play it without sounding desperate.'

Sandra kept thinking about Eric's comment: 'He's in love with you.'

She spread her scores on the piano: only one new song this afternoon. Good, she could escape early. Don't spoil everything, Billy. The flashes of irritation were more frequent lately, though at the club, Billy was always excellent – his laconic manner, his light blue eyes flashing around the audience.

Meredith and Eric stayed away from the club after that evening. Sandra was pleased – she'd rather play among strangers. Even the flower woman was welcome. Jealous? No, she wasn't.

Another smoky night: a good crowd, hard to see across the room. They left the club later than usual, into misty rain.

'I'll drive you home,' Billy said. 'You'll be absolutely safe,' he added.

'Thanks, that'd be good.' Sandra wondered how long they could continue their music partnership with this imbalance. One day, Billy would walk away…

'They were there again, those two blokes,' Billy said. 'On the right side. See if they turn up next week. They left again before we finished.'

The following Friday night the crowd was thinner. Halfway through the set, Sandra saw the two strangers come in, their faces shadowed in the low lights. As Billy predicted, they got up to go before the final song.

'I think,' Billy said, 'there's something odd about those two.'

'How do you mean?' Sandra pulled up the collar of her coat, hugging her bag to her chest.

'After we play *Winter's Day* they leave. It was the same last time.'

'Maybe they've had enough by then.'

'Can we try something next week? Play *Winter's Day* last. If that's why they leave, then we'll see who it is. Could be they're talent scouts?'

'Why would they keep coming back?'

'You're cynical sometimes, do you know that?'

A taxi cruised past and Billy waved his arm at it. As it parked by the kerb, he kissed her goodnight. 'Sweet dreams, see you Tuesday.'

Sandra never told Billy that she'd phoned his home once. And once was enough. He might love her, but it didn't stop him seeing someone, going to bed with someone else. She wasn't jealous, but there was a sensation like a stone lodged in her stomach when she thought about him, about Nick. Ha, she told herself, I should write a song about it, call it *Disappointment*.

They didn't see the strangers again. Oh well, it was hardly a mystery, probably visitors to Sydney – they'd heard the music and wandered inside, listened to a few songs, got up and left. So what?

Next rehearsal, as Sandra met Billy at the entrance to the club, he took her arm, saying, 'I'm curious. I know where some of your pieces come from – the *Mountain Valley Blues* and *Mermaid Rock*, even variations on *Song for Emilia*, and of course, our spaghetti blues—'

Here was the question she had always hoped to avoid, didn't want to answer. She shook off his hand with a non-committal shrug.

He left the question hanging as they made their way inside. Then as Sandra sat at the piano, he pounced.

'Tell me who you wrote *Winter's Day* for.' It wasn't a question, it was a demand.

'It was for a friend,' she answered, blurring the edges.

'I think you wrote it for someone special and that's why you want to play it every bloody night.'

'I told you, I wrote it for a friend. For a special *place*, if you really want to know.'

Billy gave one of his smirks. 'Nup. I bet you wrote it for some bloke.'

'Don't be funny.' She drowned any further comment with the beginning of their first piece, gratified to hear the sax come in on the beat. She wanted to tell Billy, Shut up! bothered at the same time if his question really mattered. It was beginning to feel like history.

Rain fell for several days and fewer people came to the club. So much for spring, Sandra thought, as she set up her music. The table on the right was already occupied by someone, face in the shadow.

Billy's questions at rehearsal had unnerved her, and his remarks about the two strangers who'd sat at that table a month ago, were distracting. Breathe in, she instructed herself. Count one-two-three on the breaths. Relax your shoulders. Begin the first piece... Fine.

The music flowed, and soon she'd forgotten her edginess. When they played *Misty*, again Sandra sang the words to herself in a whispered voice. Billy glanced over, nodded with approval. Everything was all right between them, thank goodness.

As he'd suggested, they kept *Winter's Day* for their final song. The figure remained at the table, but alone on this wet night.

The 'flower woman' – as Sandra nicknamed her – came out of the audience towards Billy, and as he left the stage she linked her arm through his.

Seeing Sandra's startled expression, Billy said, 'Sandra, meet Jenny.' And in a stage whisper, he added, 'we actually know each other now.'

Billy had lied to her? After the first flower-tossing episode, somehow he'd caught up with the woman, secretly, and all along... well, Sandra could hardly complain about secrets. Ha ha, *Billy Liar*.

She kissed Billy goodnight, nodded to Jenny, and watched them walk into the darkness under a single umbrella. No offer of a lift home tonight.

She'd forgotten her own umbrella, how silly – and set off at a brisk pace in the direction of the Hotel Australia.

Footsteps sounded behind her and she quickened her pace. Too gloomy to take a short-cut up Rowe Street...

She heard her name called. It could be anyone from the club: all strangers, unknown. Heart in her mouth, she turned to face whoever it was hurrying towards her.

In the random street lights, rain glistening on his hair, his face, coat flapping as he ran, boots splashing on the wet pavement – Nick Morgan!

In an instant, he'd folded his arms around her, kissed her hair, her wet cheeks, her mouth. Too stunned to respond, Sandra froze like a statue.

'Sandra—' Nick said. 'I have so much to tell you, but I was afraid—' He dropped his arms, stepped away from her, uncertain.

Finally, she was able to answer, 'You never wrote again. You never rang.' Her voice rose. 'For all I knew, you were dead.'

Nick steered her up the street and into the hotel. The foyer was busy, and he guided Sandra to a quieter corner of the lounge.

She regarded him across the table – his pale face, his shaking hands. 'Was it you at the club a few weeks ago, with whoever it was – never speaking, leaving before we finished?'

'I wanted to, believe me. I came with a mate from uni—'

'You're at uni again?'

'No, and I'm leaving tomorrow. My friend was too busy to come, but I was determined to see you tonight.'

As he ordered their coffees, she saw with sadness the hollows in his cheeks, blue patches beneath his eyes; knuckles cracked and scabbed. Nick... he looked terrible.

'I wanted to tell you, and I should've told you sooner, but with everything the way it was... I couldn't.'

Softer now, her heart no longer racing with fright and anger, she put her hand over his. 'I'm sorry for the way I reacted. I didn't know who was following me. It's not Curradeen here.'

'My fault,' Nick smiled apologetically. He took a sip of coffee. 'I wouldn't mind a splash of rum in this,' he joked. His dear, familiar smile.

'You wanted to tell me something?' Sandra asked. Something about university? Maybe he was deferring another six months. Another year.

Nick shook his head, 'No, not now.' He looked up from his coffee, glanced around the room, then as if measuring his question, he asked: 'Are you and Billy together? The way you play, you both look so good. That's why I never spoke to you. But tonight Billy left with someone—'

'We're just music partners, that's all, and it's going really well.'

Nick took her hand across the table. 'So, what about coming back to Wilga Park for a few days after your exams?'

Aware of Nick's relief at her reply about Billy, she was stunned by this surprising suggestion. Her first thought had been, What about the club, what about Billy? Billy's name again… she brushed it aside. This was a chance – perhaps a last chance – to be with Nick, to see the Morgans again. Should she ask about his family, about the drought, about Beth?

'You're sure it will it be all right – how is your mother?'

'She's not too bad,' Nick said. 'Will you come?'

He drained his coffee, put down the cup with a sharp click, waited in the silence between them for her answer.

'I guess it's only missing one rehearsal,' she finally said. 'I'll work it out.'

Sandra knew it sounded weak, but she wanted to go, she was dying to go. The old affection welled up in her as she allowed a smile. 'Late October?'

'Perfect. Any time, just give me a ring.'

Nick hailed a taxi for her, and after a fleeting kiss, he was walking fast into the rainy night.

When she arrived home, Sandra felt like yelling out down the hallway, 'I saw Nick! I'm going to Curradeen!' But in the dark and silent room, she slipped off her wet shoes and coat, threw her clothes onto a chair, and after a quick wash, she tucked herself into bed.

Never, Sandra mused… never in a million years, could I have predicted meeting Nick like that. Such a heart-ache. She pressed a finger to her lips – lips that Nick barely skimmed with a cool kiss, as if he were embarrassed. Or scared?

twelve.

As the plane circled before coming in to land, Sandra pressed her cheek to the window, saw barren paddocks deserted of stock. Like surveying an abandoned country, she thought. The plane seemed to almost touch the treetops before landing. She was tired after the exams, dispirited, already wondering if this visit was a mistake.

Nick waited by the gate, right on time, the same slight kiss on her lips. She felt uneasy – his manner was strained, the light gone from his eyes.

'We'll talk at home,' he said, putting her suitcase in the back of the ute.

The town appeared much the same as when she'd seen it months ago, although a couple of shops were closed, For Sale signs on each door. As they drove across the countryside, it opened out to an arid plain, brittle trees and clumps of saltbush lending the only colour.

During the final drive to the entrance of Wilga Park, Sandra's apprehension grew. Nick had hardly spoken, except to mutter, 'Thanks for making the trip,' which only made her feel worse. No animals, anywhere. Then as they parked at the garden gate, in the round yard close by, she spotted two horses.

With surprise, she exclaimed, 'Isn't that Toffee?'

'And Honey,' Nick gave his first real smile. 'I decided to keep her. I can care for them better here. I gave Paddy away, he's a good first horse for a kid.'

'Oh, Honey looks beautiful.'

She wanted to run and pat them both, but Nick said, 'First, a cup of tea, right? I'm parched and you must be thirsty.'

'Where are the dogs?' Sandra asked, seeing the empty kennels, chains lying loose in the dust.

'I gave the young one to a drover I met on the stock route. Trix is somewhere – she hangs about.'

He whistled shrilly through his teeth and the kelpie came, dancing around his legs. Nick smoothed her head, fondled the silky ears. 'She's a good old worker, aren't you, girl?'

The homestead seemed to crouch under a cloak of neglect. The path to the house was no more than a dusty track; the veranda needed sweeping. Inside, the rooms weighed heavy with melancholy.

Nick saw her glance about the kitchen. 'Sorry, it's a mess, but I can't keep up.' He filled the kettle with water and set two mugs on the table.

'Nick, tell me about your mother?'

Hardly breathing, she watched Nick as he turned to face her, passed her a mug of tea.

'Mum isn't coming home. She's had a couple more strokes and the care is better in Melbourne with her family. There's a nurse comes every day—' His face starting to crumble, he slumped in a chair, then looking up at Sandra again, he said, 'I shouldn't have asked you to come. It's dreadful here. The whole place, the house… my mother.'

'But she'll come back eventually, won't she?'

Nick shook his head. 'She can't speak. Her right side's no use, she can't dress or feed herself. She'd never manage. And my father—'

He looked so downcast, she decided his father's news could wait. 'When we finish our tea, can we say hello to the horses?' she suggested. Anyway, she'd rather Mr Morgan stayed in Melbourne with Beth.

Pushing back his chair, Nick opened the screen door and they walked through the garden, the yellowed grass. 'I've tried to care for the roses,' he said. 'It's probably useless, but they're tough old plants.'

'Your mother and I watered them with buckets. And look, there's some buds.'

'I'll tell her next time I phone. I ring every few days, not that there's much to say, and I'm never sure if she understands.'

The horses came to the fence, nickered, and Nick put his hand in his pocket. 'She always likes a carrot,' he said, stroking Toffee while she munched.

Sandra ran her hand down the horse's neck, enjoying the warm chaffy smell. 'The first day we met at the polocrosse you gave me a carrot for her, but I didn't know how to hold it.'

They patted the horses until Nick said, 'I've got a chook for dinner – guess I'd better go and fire up the oven. We've got an electric stove now, better than the old Aga in summer.' Again, his quick smile. 'Mum would've loved it.'

Preparing the chicken for the roasting tin, he said, 'I'm having a beer while I do this. Want one?'

'Mmm, I don't really drink beer—'

'Wine, then? Lemonade?'

'Yes, please. A glass of wine.'

'You can choose. There's several bottles in the fridge, bottom shelf.'

Nick grinned when Sandra showed him the label on her choice. 'Ha, one of Dad's best whites. You've got expensive tastes, young lady.'

'That's what your father called me after I played the piano.'

'Last winter – you made him happy, I remember.'

While Nick fixed the chicken, surrounding it with sliced vegetables, she watched his hands, enjoying his brisk movements, the practised way he dealt with it.

'You won't get anything fresher than this,' he slid the tin into the oven. 'Killed this morning.'

'You did that?'

'Chopped, plucked and roasted by me. Let me know if you find the odd feather.'

While the chicken cooked, they took their drinks to sit on the veranda.

'These boards have heard a lot of talk over the decades.' Nick raised his glass, 'Here's cheers. You've no idea how good it is you're here, Sandra. You've done me a big, big favour.'

A *favour*… that wasn't how it felt to Sandra. There were a lot of unanswered questions, and one by one, she intended to find out the answers. Eight months without a word from Nick and then he showed up – secretly – at the club. Begged her, yes, really it felt like begging, to visit Wilga Park. He could have told her the story in Sydney. There was no reason for her to be here, in this atmosphere of desolation.

'Cheers,' she responded, at a loss for anything else to say. A lone cricket scuttled across the floor.

'I haven't told you,' Nick said, 'how much I liked hearing my song at the club. Actually, it was a bit of a shock.'

'Billy spotted you a while ago. He said "two strangers" but I'd never have guessed it was you.'

Nick looked into his glass. 'Ha, sorry about that. Whenever I had a gut-full of Dad's orders, I'd just take off, but I could only ever stay overnight. And then, watching you and Billy—' She heard his long exhalation of breath. 'I seem to be saying sorry a lot,' he added. 'Well, I am sorry. For a lot of things.'

Evening was closing in. Beyond the peppertrees, horizon and sky merged in a last golden haze. In another month it would be officially summer. Nick jumped up several times to check the dinner, put knives and forks on the table. In the centre, he placed a small vase with sprigs of yellow flowers. 'Weeds,' he commented. 'That's about all that grows now. We call these bobbliejinks.'

He poured a glass of wine for himself, topped up Sandra's. They ate and drank, and when Sandra found a tiny white quill stuck in the chicken leg, she plucked it out with a giggle.

'I couldn't cook a roast dinner if I tried,' she admitted. 'This is really the best chook I've ever eaten.'

'Thanks. Mum thought I should know how to cook, for when I was here by myself.'

'You're sometimes here alone?'

'Yes, whenever my parents went to wool or sheep sales, and I stayed home. And when Mum went to Melbourne to see her family, I'd cook for Dad and me.'

After a dessert of icecream and jelly, they took their glasses and the bottle and went to the lounge room. Nick lit a candle, pushed wide open the doors to the veranda.

He raised the lid of the radiogram. 'Since my mother left,' he said, 'I've been going through her classical records. I wish I'd taken more notice when I was growing up; I mostly listened to pop like the Delltones and Buddy Holly, though Mum and I got to like The Beatles—'

'The Beatles, too!'

He slipped a record onto the turntable. 'This is one of her favourites – a Saint-Saëns concerto – she reckoned the piano was like horses cantering.'

'You told me you learned piano for a while—'

'For a while. Kids at school gave me a hard time so I quit.'

Nick patted the cushions for Sandra to sit beside him. A crooked smile at her over the top of his glass, he said, 'I like to sit here every evening with my feet up, and watch the country going to hell.'

Nick's ironical remark was so unexpected, Sandra had no immediate reply.

'All the galahs have cleared out,' he added.

Sensing that behind him lurked a black cloud. she put her feet next to his on the foot-stool. Perhaps this was the moment to ask, and Nick had just given her the cue.

'Nick, there's something—' she began.

'Yes, there is.' Voice harsh with sudden bitterness, he said, 'I was crazy to think you should come. It was selfish. I'm by myself and your parents don't know that. You shouldn't be here. We'll change the ticket tomorrow and you can go home.'

She chose to ignore his plea that she should leave. 'You haven't mentioned your father, when's he coming home?'

Nick's shoulders shuddered as if he'd dropped a heavy bale of hay. 'Okay, I didn't know how to tell you... it's like this: the last time my father decided we couldn't carry the rest of the sheep, he shot all but fifty—'

He was rushing to speak, his words tumbling. 'Fifty sheep, the best of the best – with the mob on agistment, all that's left from three generations of the Morgan stud.'

Sandra remembered the day Harry Morgan returned from shooting the first sheep: the look on his face... the look on Nick's face after he'd bulldozed them into the burial ground. She wanted to weep – for the family, the poor sheep, the whole helpless situation.

'Oh, that's terrible for your father—'

'He didn't speak for days, just sat in his office. Sometimes I looked in to check how he was, and he'd be sitting, staring at nothing—'

Nick suddenly got up, returning with another bottle of wine. 'I'm not only working my way through Mum's records, I'm working my way through Dad's cellar.' He flourished the bottle. '*Chianti classico*, drink it anywhere.'

He drew the cork, filling their glasses. 'My mates are all beer drinkers, but my folks liked a glass of wine with dinner. I got used to it.'

Accustomed to seeing him with a cigarette in his hand, Sandra asked, 'You don't smoke any more?'

Nick gave a grim smile, lip turned down. 'I got to hate the smell of Dad's cigarettes. Gave it up.'

The music flowed around them – smooth arpeggios up and down the keyboard – disturbing and lovely at the same time. The candle guttered, and they continued to sit in the darkening room.

'I tried, Sandra, I really tried,' Nick said. 'I wanted to convince Dad I'd stay here, help the place get back on its feet, build up the stud again when the season changed.' He bunched his fist. 'My father didn't believe me. Mum had gone, she'd never return to the life they'd led together. He felt he'd gone sour, wasted his life... wasted himself.'

'But how do you know he felt like that?'

Nick swivelled to look at her. 'He told me. He stood over there at the fireplace, and he told me. He said he'd quietly put Wilga Park on the market several months ago, and signed the expected proceeds over to me with enough to look after Mum for the rest of her life. That's when I took off to Sydney the first time, and went to your club with my mate.'

Heaving an enormous sigh, the words burst from his lips: 'I can't put it off any longer, I've got to tell you. My father's gone.'

'What? Where's he gone?'

Nick didn't immediately answer. He gulped his wine, gazing fixedly at the floor. Then, as if he dredged up the words from some wretched place, he said: 'He's gone, Sandra, he's dead.'

Shocked, she took his hand, held it tightly while Nick stared into the night. 'Oh, Nick, I'm so sorry. What happened?'

'He shot himself. He drove to the woolshed and *shot* himself.'

Sandra caught her breath. Harry Morgan, tough to the end, must have wept to lose the pride and joy of his life. But was it so terrible he had to give up and take his own life? She couldn't understand it. Surely there was always tomorrow?

'That's the saddest thing I ever heard,' she whispered. She reached a hand to him, touched his shoulder, felt the tension in his body. 'When—?'

'Two months ago. *Do your best, son*, he told me, and slammed out of the house. He left me to go searching for him when he didn't come in for dinner.'

Two months of stored grief: Nick wept silently, head in his hands. 'The woolshed, the damn bloody woolshed ... where his heart was, you know? His whole love for this place.'

'And you've been here all alone, ever since? What about friends, your neighbours?'

'Everyone came. Ladies bearing casseroles.' Nick wiped his eyes with the back of his hand. 'Dad did everything except bury himself. I did that for him, in the Curradeen cemetery. Oh, he got a good send off, so many people—'

Still shocked, Sandra saw that Nick's mouth had set hard. He laughed, without humour. 'The old man gave me the property, knowing I didn't want it. How's that for a bad joke?'

'He must've loved you—'

'He loved my mother, I know that. But I took after her, not him, and that was his greatest disappointment. He thought he could change me, until she persuaded him to let me go.'

'What will happen now?'

'I need to be gone from here. An English company's buying the place. It's all but done, thank god.'

Nick poured another glass and they leaned back on the cushions, listening to the more and more fretful concerto.

'I've tried to make a plan. I want to visit Mum again. She doesn't understand that Dad's gone. I've taken all her clothes to her family, her precious things. I don't know for how long... my grandparents are in their eighties.' She heard his small sigh, his anxiety. 'I'll tell you more about it tomorrow.'

'You want me to leave tomorrow, you said—'

'No. Please stay. Maybe you can help me.'

Help Nick? How could she help him? To pack up several lifetimes of the Morgans was impossible. She had to be home by Friday—

As if he'd read her thoughts, Nick said, 'You've got to get home. Anyway, the sale's walk in, walk out. There's debts to settle, the mob on agistment, finalizing the stud records. Antique dealers have already crawled over the house like so many leeches.'

The record had ended without them noticing. Nick went to the french doors, stepped onto the veranda. 'Come outside,' he called. 'The moon's up.'

A sliver of moon illuminated the homestead, the desiccated garden, the bone-dry land magically transformed by shades of silver. Low on the horizon, the Southern Cross pricked the sky. The kelpie snuffled around their feet, licking hands.

'I wanted Trix to come in the house and keep me company,' Nick said. 'But she wouldn't. A working dog, through and through.'

They meandered through the gate, beyond the rosemary hedge, the peppertrees, and along the dirt road. Sandra breathed in the smell of eucalypts carried on the warm night air, tilted her head to gaze at the bright stars.

'Part of me will always love this place,' Nick murmured. 'Part of me will be heartbroken to leave. You see, I could always come home. As long as Mum and Dad were here, it was my home too.'

She heard the immeasurable sadness in his voice, slipped her arm through his. 'You'll make a new home, Nick. You'll build your house, and it will be yours, for as long as you choose.'

'Tomorrow,' he said. 'We can talk tomorrow.'

Sandra knew where to find the guest room, even in the dark hallway. Her suitcase was there, half unpacked, but she hadn't done more than wash her face since arriving.

Nick had kissed her goodnight – almost absentmindedly, she thought, as if he'd got lost down some crevasse of despair. She put her head on the pillow, pulled up the sheet, felt a wave of nausea. Too much wine.

Overwhelmed, tears trickled down each cheek, tears she'd held onto while she listened to Nick's story: Harry Morgan's death, Beth, who she'd never see again. Strange to think about it, she was encircled by people who loved music, people for whom music formed part of their lives... and Nick, alone for weeks, surviving on his memory of better days. She heard the click and rustle of the dog on the veranda. She was going to be sick.

Leaning over the toilet, her stomach heaved and she vomited. Rinsing her mouth, she spat into the bowl. A long drink of water made her feel better. Her face in the mirror, tired eyes. You've been awake too long, she told her reflection.

Stretched out again in bed, her head was a jumble of thoughts. Emilia hadn't written – she must've known. Nick had left his father at home and come to Sydney – wanting to speak, misunderstanding Billy. Until the last time. She figured it had to be soon after his father killed himself. She did her best to shut away her vision of Harry Morgan as he levelled the rifle, the ghastly wound for Nick to discover.

Down the hallway, Nick lay in his narrow bed. Along the veranda... he'd come to her that night in January, through the french doors, to tell her about his mother's illness. Tonight she wanted to be close to him. Be brave, she told herself, he can only shoo you away.

Tip-toeing, Sandra gently pushed her doors open-wide, stepped onto the boards, felt the fine veneer of dust on her soles. Nick's bedroom doors were open and she entered, dimly focussing on the moonlit outlines of furniture: desk, chair, cupboard, bed.

Very gently, she sat on the bed, then carefully swung her legs up, to lie beside him. No sheet between them, Nick lay bare-skinned on the bed, wearing only boxer shorts.

Awake, he put his arm around her shoulders. 'I was thinking about you. I wanted you to come, and here you are.'

She kissed his lips, felt his sleepy response. 'I'm smashed. We drank too much.'

'I just threw up,' Sandra whispered.

'That's romantic.' She felt the tremor of his laugh. 'Stay here, if it's not too hot?'

They heard the heavy sound of the dog as she settled by the door. 'Trix is happy. I'm happy...' his voice trailed off, and she knew he'd slipped into a deep sleep.

Shifting herself gently off Nick's arm, she nestled against his shoulder. This is what happiness might feel like, she thought – to find contentment in the midst of sorrow.

And she realized how deeply she cared for Nick... she loved this man. Not the childish crush of years ago, but built on a quiet friendship with shared conversations over years. There was a part of Nick that continued to love the bush, his horses, and yet there was the side of him that needed the city with all that it offered. This is what she shared with him too.

Eyes closed, she remembered words she'd told herself, long ago: we will be like two stars circling about each other, drawn together – a double star.

But again she heard his words: *I wish it could be different.*

Very early in the morning when Sandra awoke, she was alone in the bed, a tangle of sheets on the floor. Distant clattering noises came from the kitchen. This wasn't how the stories went in books and films. Well, what had she expected? She padded along the veranda to the guest room, filled with conflicting thoughts. Perhaps she was imagining it – perhaps his kisses blew away with the dust. Already she wanted to leave, but she would stay for the allotted time, try to be cheerful, and then...

Nick put two plates of bacon and eggs on the table. 'Sleep well? I didn't want to disturb you too early.' He buttered a pile of toast. 'Thanks for listening last night. It was good to talk about it to someone like you.'

Someone like you... 'But you told me you've spoken to friends here, people who know your family?'

'Sort of. But it's not the same. I told you once, you've got an understanding that's deeper. I've never been able to talk to the people around here about anything except sheep and wool and my future on Wilga Park. No one supported me to leave. No one except finally, my mother, and no one could figure out her decision either.'

'It seems simple enough to me.'

A shadow passed across his face. 'It's all over now, this is the end play.'

When Sandra didn't speak, he said, 'Eat up, while it's hot.'

Breakfast finished, Nick collected the bucket of scraps saying, 'Come and we'll feed the chooks. They'll be all of a flutter, wondering which one gets her head chopped off today.'

'Noo, please don't do it while I'm here!'

'Don't worry, I'll make something else for dinner. There's plenty of chops in the fridge.'

Chickens clustered expectantly at the gate – brown, white and speckled heads craning, stepping impatiently on each other's feet – until Nick threw the scraps among them, sparking a frantic scramble. 'The company's bought the stud, so they're welcome to the chooks too, if they want them.' He topped up the feed and water troughs, toeing a pushy chicken out of the way. 'Sorry, girls, I can't take you with me.'

Sandra emerged from the tin shelter with several eggs. Determined to make the best of it, she announced cheerfully, 'More eggs for breakfast!' She watched as Nick opened the gate for the chickens to roam, his face impassive.

'What's the next job?' she offered.

'Checking the pumps, but we'll have a cup of tea first. I already threw a load in the washing machine.'

Nick filled the kettle while Sandra set out cups, choosing the blue willow pattern. Concerned that he would be caught between the sale and his purchase of a property, she asked, 'Where will you go when you have to leave?'

'Well, I can't go back to the college – I'll have the horses and Trix, all my belongings. Or ...' he gave a wry smile, 'what if the vice-chancellor lets me put my horses on the college oval? I could set up a tent, take the chooks with me. What do you think?'

She pictured the oval scattered with tents and horses like a little circus. 'That would be fun, with chickens running everywhere. But seriously, Nick, what will you do?'

'If I can't buy a place, then I'll rent somewhere. And if I'm lucky enough to find the right property, I'll get a caravan while I build my house.'

Nick drank his tea, his gaze far away into the distance.

'Who'll live here when the sale's gone through?' Sandra persisted.

He shook his head, 'I don't want to think about it. The big pastoral companies put a manager on, unless it's a family business. A family would be nice, people who'd care for Wilga Park like us.'

He squeezed her shoulder, 'I'll work it out, don't worry about me.'

Nick carried the laundry basket heavy with work clothes to the clothesline, draping dozens of socks on the wire fence where in the hot sun they'd be dry in an hour. Later, wearing Mrs Morgan's straw sunhat, Sandra folded everything into the basket.

With each shirt she unpegged from the line, she continued to wonder at Nick's manner towards her. Yes, he was caring, considerate, affectionate. She heard that horrid little chorus *I wish it could be different.* Clenching her teeth, she resolved to get used

to being just a friend, try not to care too much, not to be in love…
sleep in the guest room—

Carrying the basket inside, she met Nick at the kitchen door.

Oblivious to her mood, 'Team work!' he declared, a shine in his eyes. 'You're a good worker.'

A full day cleaning the house, while music blaring from the radiogram filled every room. Concertos, sonatas, symphonies – Nick played them all, and when he'd exhausted every one, he played them again, throwing an occasional Buddy Holly or Delltones into the mix. From the far end of the house, she heard him singing, *Get a Little Dirt on Your Hands,* and smiled at the insanity – the pleasure of these final hours at Wilga Park; the small emotional ache in her heart that never went away.

At the veranda door, Nick, leaning on the broad broom: 'Mum would love it,' he said. 'She always played her records quietly, while she read or sewed. She didn't want to disturb Dad in his office.'

'Your father didn't like it?'

'No, he liked other stuff. Military bands, for god's sake. Really, they were a strange couple. I guess my mother got swept up in the romance of this place, the history. It would've been an adventure to come here from Melbourne.'

'When we met, you told me how your great-grandmother arrived, with the first piano in the district on a bullock cart.'

'You've got a good memory. I better be careful what I say.' His crooked smile again.

'How did your parents meet?'

'Oh, matchmaking friends. Mum came up from Melbourne for a ball. But they loved each other, all the same.'

The long hallway seemed surprisingly light, the walls bare. Hands on hips, Sandra surveyed the hall, thinking how strange it looked without the old gilt frames, the whiskery faces of Wilga Park's pioneers. She shoved the vacuum cleaner into the cupboard as Nick came in from endlessly sweeping the veranda.

'You've taken down the grandfather paintings—'

'I got tired of their accusing eyes every time I walked past,' Nick replied. 'But it was my father who put the place on the market, not me.'

'Will you keep the willow-pattern china on the dresser? Maybe the dresser too?'

'Sure. I'll keep Mum's good china and her crystal glasses. And great-grandmother's silver.'

'What about the furniture, isn't there anything you want?'

'Not a lot, there isn't. My desk—'

'Your house plan has a big kitchen, so you'll need a table.'

He surprised her with a kiss, one-two on each cheek. 'And yes, before you ask me, I'm keeping the piano.'

After lunch, when the temperature edged higher, Nick sat at the desk, his house plans spread before him. Intrigued, Sandra watched as he drew a copy, omitting some details, adding others. His hand was firm, setting the outline of a very old ambition.

She inspected his original drawings: the detailed design with its satisfying proportions and colourful features, the wide protecting eaves, its northern windows. He'd illustrated the courtyard with flagstones, carefully positioned trees.

'You could be an artist, full-time.' She tapped the drawing with a fingertip. 'Like the lovely drawing you gave me and the dust storm picture.'

Nick gave her a quick smile, 'I used to think about it, then I got interested in designing houses.'

'Do both? Everyone likes a painting of their own home.'

'Full of ideas, aren't you. Maybe…'

The bobbliejinks had withered overnight. Venturing beyond the garden to the paddock, Sandra discovered white paper daisies for the little vase.

Tonight Nick had drawn the cork on another bottle of his father's best wine, filled crystal glasses, held a match to the candles. Sliding their plates onto the table, he announced, 'Grilled chops and three veg, my mother's favourite.'

They'd worked till seven and the evening was warm. Trix settled at the open door, her nose on the step, brown eyes on Nick as he reached now and then to fill their glasses, the wine soft and easy. Sandra felt contented to enjoy this mellow evening, perhaps the last time she'd see Nick before their world turned upside-down. He'd spoken confidently about his plans but she still considered it a gamble where he might be end up with no home and nowhere to go.

Her thoughts drifted to the club, her music for Friday night. She'd play again the songs that brought Nick running after her that winter night, end with *Winter's Day* – no matter what, it would always be his song.

Nick put on another record, topped up their glasses. A mixture of music played: sonatas, Strauss, Beatles, Billy Holiday. The candles melted and dripped, creating patterns on their silver holders.

Sandra's eyelids were heavy and her legs ached from working all day. I must've walked a hundred miles – sweeping, dusting, packing Beth's china into boxes. She had no idea how long they'd sat together on the couch, her legs draped across Nick's stretched out on the footstool, when from far away she heard his voice.

'Play the piano for me? Play *Clair de Lune*, play my song, anything you like.—'

'It's so late—'

'Doesn't matter... you're the midnight pianist, right?'

Waking up in the guest room fully clothed under a sheet, Sandra couldn't recollect going to bed, vaguely aware that she hadn't played the piano.

Swathed in Mrs Morgan's dressing gown, she went out to the veranda. Morning sky reflected pale pink, a glow of sun beyond the rim; then as she watched, up rose the giant fiery sphere like she'd never seen before. Never been so far west.

Nick handed her a mug of tea. 'G'day, sleepy-head.'

'Thanks for putting me to bed.' Sandra sipped her tea, amused at the thought of a tipsy Nick carrying her through the darkened house, tucking her into bed.

He let down a blind to cut the glare, and they sat in cane chairs sipping tea while the day developed: a brief chorus of birdsong, fading to silence. Trix lay down with a lazy thump, stretched out, nose on her paws, eyes steadfastly on Nick.

'It's going to be very hot today. Not a good sign for summer,' Nick poured more tea, then leaned back in the chair, cradling his mug.

'This is my plan, so far. Despite the drought, it's a good price for Wilga Park, enough to care for Mum and buy me a few acres. Big enough for some horses, somewhere between the mountains and the sea. I'll build my house, and then I'll see.'

'The plan you showed me?'

'Teenage dreams... but I know what I want. And I'll switch from architecture. I don't want to build skyscrapers and houses for millionaires, I just want to build homes – comfortable, beautiful homes, and I don't need a six year degree to do it. My father and I built the stockman's cottage when I was only seventeen.'

'Sounds good,' Sandra said, watching the sun rise, streaking the horizon with colours. She looked at him, trying to see behind his expression. He was relaxed this morning, his shoulders loose, his mouth without the tightness he'd worn last night.

She wanted to believe it was because she was here. Like magic, one moment she was playing piano in the club, the next, sitting on a veranda watching the sun come up, watching Nick...

Reckless, she reached across to him, touched his shoulder, touched his lean, strong forearm where it rested on the chair, the fine hairs; ran a finger along the veins on his hand. Who cares, she thought, I love him and I can't help it. It was hard not to cry.

Tomorrow, she would say goodbye to the horses and Trix, Nick would put her suitcase in the back of the ute and they'd take the road into Curradeen. Aware of gathering tears, she patted a pocket of her dressing gown, searching for a handkerchief. As if Trix knew, the dog gave Sandra a nudge with her nose, a wag of the tail.

Nick's quiet voice brought Sandra back to the veranda.

'Touch me like that,' he said, 'and I'll never let you go home.'

Cheeks burning, she felt the rapid drumming of her heart. 'I may not want to go home,' she confided, playing with his fingers. 'I have to, of course, but I may not want to.'

'Sandra?'

She waited for him to speak, tried to fathom the question in his eyes.

'Build my house with me, you and me, together... Marry me?'

Unable to speak, she knew he could read her response, saw her happiness reflected in his face.

Nick put his mug on the floor. Taking her hands in his, he kissed her forehead, her cheeks. 'When I met you as a fourteen-year old girl,' he said, 'I never imagined you'd be standing here with me, like this—' He lifted a strand of hair, let it slip silken through his fingers. 'Darling, sweet Sandra... I love you. I think I've always loved you.'

His fingertips traced the line of her throat, her shoulders... eyes closed, he stroked each arm, caressed her waist, her hips, as if sensing the elements of her body through the cloth, sunlight catching curves and shadows.

Holding Nick's face in her hands as she kissed him, she heard the quick intake of his breath; heard her own words – words she had once thought impossible to say:

'Dearest, darling Nick,' she whispered. 'I've loved you forever.'

And she knew it was perfect, it was natural, for them to be standing together like this, in the warmth of the early morning radiance.

In the evening, leaving their dinner dishes in the sink, they sat on the couch, shoulder to shoulder, faces turned towards the veranda, the merest breeze. Trix with her nose on the step, still determined not to come inside.

'This is like a new chapter, isn't it?' Sandra said. 'A realization of everything you've ever wanted: living closer to Sydney—'

'Closer to you.' Nick kissed the back of her neck. 'And when you want to be with me, you'll be close to what you want and need – your studies, your own pathway.'

For a while they sat quietly, fingers interlaced, breathing the familiar dry scent of the bush. Yes, all that was important, but so was her life with him. Their paths had criss-crossed down different ways and then entwined, just as Aunt Meredith said so long ago.

'You're my pathway, too.' She kissed his mouth, loving his tenderness, the blaze of happiness. A few more hours – it was as if she could already hear the engines of the morning plane. Unbelievable to think she would never come to this house again, this home.

The idea bloomed all of a sudden: 'Guess what? I'm going to play the piano – one last time before I leave tomorrow.'

Glimmer of light from a thin moon filtered across the veranda and through the study window. No need for a lamp, she could have played these pieces with her eyes shut.

Opening the lid of the piano – Beth's piano – a moment's hesitation, her fingers suspended over the keys, thoughts swirling... first, *Song for Emilia*, because there'll always be a place for Emmy in my life. We'll see each other again, I promise. Calmly and surely, her fingers found the five-bar opening adagio leading to the melody, and in an instant and for this special evening, she changed the urgent crescendo chorus to a gentle ripple of quavers, until she'd twice-played all the notes of the melody... this single variation, barely five singing minutes as it drifted soft as a breeze to the last quiet chords.

With a glance at Nick, into the stillness of the room she began *Winter's Day*. From the first notes, faces floated before her: Dear Beth, so unexpectedly ill... Harry Morgan, lost now and always. Yesterday she'd ridden with Nick as far as the creek, since dried to stones, Honey walking obediently beside Toffee... a sudden change in the beat: allegretto for two horses released and free, racing into the dusk, tails streaming... and finally, eyes wet with unexpected tears, she played the cadence – reflection of the peace that lay across the house right this moment, the peace of midnight – Nick, motionless at the door, regarding her from across the darkening room.

A grey dawn light crept into the bedroom. Sandra turned her head to see Nick's sleeping form beside her, his dear face, one arm lying across her hip. She craned her neck to see the clock: the hands had stopped at 4.30. How much longer before they had to get up?

With her small movement to draw up the sheet against the early morning cool, she felt something delicate slither across her neck, swiftly put a hand to her throat to stop whatever it was, touched the metallic trickle of a thin chain.

At her involuntary flinch, Nick's eyes opened. A slow smile, and he murmured, 'Ah, you found it. You were so fast asleep you didn't stir.'

She held the pendant in her open palm, in the faint light saw an opal on a fine chain. Holding it to her cheek, she looked at Nick in wonder.

'For the lady I love,' he said. 'From that shop you like in Rowe Street – black opal, white gold. When you told me you'd come in October, I took a chance—'

She put her finger on his lips. 'Nick, it's the most beautiful thing… I'll always treasure it.'

'And I'll always treasure you, darling girl.'

Faces flushed with sleep, they hugged each other, laughing at themselves in Nick's baggy old singlets, Nick holding her almost unbearably close, heart against heart.

♪

Finale:

They didn't speak on the drive to the airport under a clear morning sky: a light breeze, glint of silver on the plane as it made its final approach.

Nick enfolded her in his arms, and Sandra bent her face into his shirt, cheek against his chest. He kissed her forehead, the tip of her nose, then long and lovingly he kissed her lips. Returning this sweet last kiss, she vowed, after today I'll never say goodbye again, never ever...

'Please ring me now and then? I hate to think of you all alone with no one to help.'

Nick touched his finger to a tear on her cheek. 'I'll be fine. Neighbours and friends will rally round. They won't see me stuck.'

The plane came to a halt, propellers slowly winding down. Sandra's suitcase was already loaded onto the luggage cart. Only three other passengers this morning, so boarding would be quick.

Her hands slipped free from his, but so hard to walk away. She turned to look back, engrave Nick's image on her heart as he stood, felt hat tipped on its customary angle, one arm raised in farewell, solitary beside the ute.

In the dazzle of sunrise, he'd whispered into her hair, 'I think I've always loved you—'

Her *Nick Nick Nicholas Nick*. Swallowing tears, Sandra waved a hand in response then stepped into the plane. The hostess motioned her to find a seat and the door clamped shut.

She heard the increased power of the engines, propellers spinning invisibly as the plane turned to taxi along the runway.

Notes

El Rocco: Australia's oldest jazz cellar, established in Kings Cross in 1955 by Arthur James

A.Mus.A.: Associate Diploma in Music, Australia

The Book of Lies, Aleister Crowley. Published London, 1913.
'*Do what thou wilt*': from *The Book of Lies*, Aleister Crowley.
Toujours Fidèle: French perfume by D'Orsay (translation: Always Faithful)
Billy Liar: 1963 film directed by John Schlesinger
Misty: composed by Erroll Garner, 1954 (lyrics added later by Johnny Burke)
Walk On By: song composed by Burt Bacharach, lyrics by Hal David, originally recorded by Dionne Warwick in 1964.

Enrique Granados: *Mazurka, from Escenas románticas (*Eric L'estrange on piano at the party)
Frédéric Chopin: *Nocturne in C minor*, Op.48, No.1
Ludwig van Beethoven: *Sonata No. 8 in C minor*, Op. 13 (Pathétique)
Camille Saint Saëns: *Concerto No.4 in C minor*, Op. 44

www.ingramcontent.com/pod-product-compliance
Lightning Source LLC
LaVergne TN
LVHW041620070426
835507LV00008B/359